PRACTICAL
DESIGN
SOLUTIONS AND STRATEGIES

W9-BRM-521

PRACTICAL DESIGN

SOLUTIONS AND STRATEGIES

**Key Advice
for Sound
Construction
from
*Fine Woodworking***

The Taunton Press

essentials of woodworking

Front cover photo by Boyd Hagan
Back cover illustration by Michael Gellatly
Back cover photos by Sloan Howard (top right) and Jonathan Binzen (bottom)

© 2000 by The Taunton Press, Inc.
All rights reserved.

Printed in the United States of America
10 9 8 7 6 5 4 3 2 1

BOOKS & VIDEOS

for fellow enthusiasts

The Taunton Press, Inc., 63 South Main Street, PO Box 5506,
Newtown, CT 06470-5506
e-mail: tp@taunton.com

Distributed by Publishers Group West

Library of Congress Cataloging-in-Publication Data
Practical design : solutions and strategies / key advice for sound
construction from Fine woodworking.
p.   cm.—(Essentials of Woodworking)
Includes index.
ISBN 1-56158-344-8
1. Furniture design. 2. Furniture making. I. Series.
TT196.P73   2000
684.1'04—dc21   99-047526

About Your Safety
Working with wood is inherently dangerous. Using hand or power tools improperly or ignoring
standard safety practices can lead to permanent injury or even death. Don't try to perform operations you
learn about here (or elsewhere) unless you're certain they are safe for you. If something about an
operation doesn't feel right, don't do it. Look for another way. We want you to enjoy the craft,
so please keep safety foremost in your mind whenever you're working with wood.

*"Many things difficult
to design prove easy
to performance"*

—SAMUEL JOHNSON, *RASSELAS*

CONTENTS

INTRODUCTION

Design is a dirty word among most furniture makers. A woodworker who proudly tells guests "I design all my own furniture" and asks if they'd like to see some of it will surely elicit a rush for the exit. That's because furniture design as a concept conjures up images of brightly painted chairs without seats or legs, tables with undulating tops and legs that wander recklessly before they hit the floor, and other sculptural "statements" that need a lot of explaining to understand, not to mention use.

Playful and artistic furniture design, however, is not the only kind. In fact, it's a rare type. It might come as a surprise, but all woodworkers must be designers to some degree. To design is to simply make a plan or build according to a plan. Design describes everything from thinking up and executing a grumpy dolphin in zebrawood to thinking through and executing a Shaker table. Cut lists, drawings, and even learned strategies for making parts are all evidence that design runs through everything woodworkers do. Without conscious design, furniture making simply couldn't happen.

Designing in its everyday sense is the problem-solving process most woodworkers love. It starts with pie-in-the-sky explorations of all the possibilities. How long of a table? What wood? What type of legs? How should they be made? Then the process becomes grounded in experience and practical realities. A 4-in.-thick bird's-eye maple dining table might be a pretty cool idea, but try to find 16/4 bird's-eye boards, the money for them, or the strength to lift them onto a tablesaw. From a sound, practical design comes the details of the execution. How should the top be attached to the apron? All these aspects need solutions, and every time a woodworker finds one, he proves he's a good designer.

This book collects the best material on practical, everyday design from *Fine Woodworking* and *Home Furniture* magazines. Professional and amateur woodworkers alike were asked to write about their strategies and solutions to particular design problems. Their many years of experience have yielded a thorough knowledge of the possible ways any one task can be accomplished. These solutions have been distilled here as design strategies for every woodworker, whether they consider themselves designers or not.

ONE

Conceiving Your Projects

All furniture designs, at one point or another, came out of the imaginations of woodworkers. The cabriole leg hasn't always been around, nor have table aprons that are mortised into legs. Someone had to think them up. From a distance, thinking up unique furniture from the broad cloth of the imagination appears a monumental task. After all, few woodworkers are Chippendales. The popularity of furniture plans and the large number of woodworkers who meticulously reproduce existing designs attest to this fear of design. Leave design to the experts and let me just make things is the mantra.

An ancient saying goes "there is nothing new under the sun." With this perspective, the monumental nature of an original design deflates. No new design is ever purely imagined, because the imagination simply collects experience and information and reprocesses it into new forms. All new designs have roots in previous designs, and those designs have roots in others. Chippendale did not start from scratch, but from the Queen Anne style. And Queen Anne grew out of other styles.

No one will ever say that coming up with a beautiful, original style design for a piece of furniture is easy, but it's within every woodworker's reach. The work takes time, a lot of thought, some strategies to help the thought processes, lots of experience with other furniture designs, and more time after that. Bill Keyser and John Gallagher offer some strategies for creating good designs, such as sketching to keep a visual record. Original design takes time, but when done well, the rewards are tremendous: You will have created something truly unique.

It's easy to forget that the strategies Keyser and Gallagher offer don't have to be applied as a whole to create a completely new design. These same strategies can be useful to change only a foot or base on a pre-existing design. This piecemeal approach to conceiving furniture can be as simple as adding a curve where there was a taper before. And before you realize it, you're designing in no different a manner than the best of them.

WHERE DESIGNS ARE BORN

by Bill Keyser

Design "travel logs." Sketchbooks like these, belonging to the author, are not only a way to get to a design, but they also become a record of the journey.

Sketching is a wonderful tool. It's a time for visual brainstorming, exploring, developing and refining forms and ideas. For many designers the sketch is where furniture is born.

A sketchbook is valuable because it is a place to let ideas flow and evolve from a raw concept to a resolved design. Like a travel journal, a sketchbook becomes a record of your progress as a designer. As forms are recorded, the sketchbook lives on as an archive of ideas to inform and inspire. A previously rejected sketch, when reexamined years later, may contain the germ of a successful design.

Making time to sketch

Sketching must be an ongoing activity if you're going to be a designer. While building one piece, you must be sketching the

next project or two. You have to make sketching a priority and schedule time to do it. Write it into your planner, or put it on your to-do list and stick to it.

There is no ideal time to sketch; you simply must find the time that works best for you. It might be the first thing you do in the morning, before your mind becomes cluttered by the demands of the day. Or it could be at day's end, when you're dog-tired, which is often the time a winning idea presents itself. Idle time, in the doctor's waiting room or at the theater before the movie begins, can offer good sketching opportunities.

Start with short sessions, about a half-hour once or twice a day. Do this for several days in a row, if time permits (I find that short, intense bursts of sketching are more productive than marathon sessions). Once you have settled on a concept, you can spend longer periods of time working out construction details and proportions of the piece, and making measured drawings.

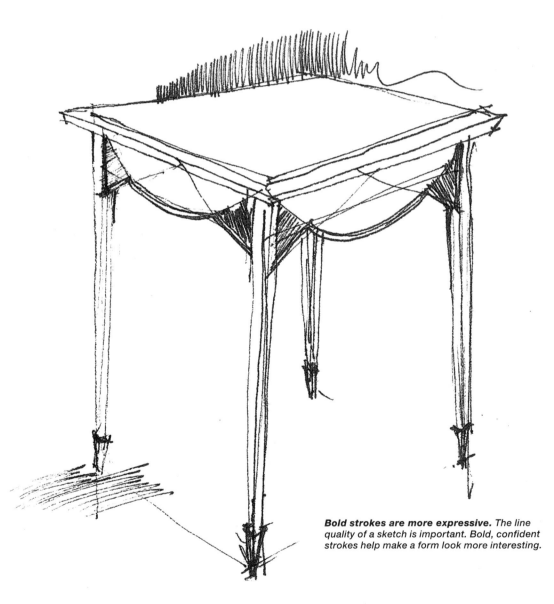

Bold strokes are more expressive. *The line quality of a sketch is important. Bold, confident strokes help make a form look more interesting.*

Setting up a sketchbook

You can sketch on just about anything. Paper napkins and the back of envelopes can be used to record a fleeting idea, and this is fine if you are caught unprepared. But an organized approach will be more professional and productive.

Some people use ruled or graph paper because they feel the grid helps when freehanding straight lines and in getting proportions right. I've found that ruled paper can become a crutch that inhibits not only the drawings but also the ideas.

Probably the best material to start with is blank, opaque, white paper available in different sizes and bindings. Stitch-bound books are the most durable, but the pages are difficult to remove, and the book doesn't fold back on itself. The spiral-bound sketchbooks can be folded in half, making them convenient for sketching in cramped quarters. The gummed tablets are the least durable, and they don't fold, but you can remove pages easily. This is an advantage if you work on more than one project at a time. You can remove sketches to hang them on the wall at the end of a brainstorming session, so you can see all the concepts and variations at a glance. You may want to mat, frame and display favorite sketches.

The size of the sketchbook is important. Pocket-sized sketchbooks allow you to take them everywhere. Larger pages encourage rapid-fire, sequential thinking on a single sheet and allow room for more detailed renderings. I use different sizes, depending on the kind of drawing I'm doing.

Warm-up exercises to get you started

Before you start drawing, orient yourself to your sketchbook as if you are standing before a painting: Your lines of sight should be perpendicular to the page. Looking down on you and your sketchbook, it should be oriented on axis with your body, not angled as if you're writing.

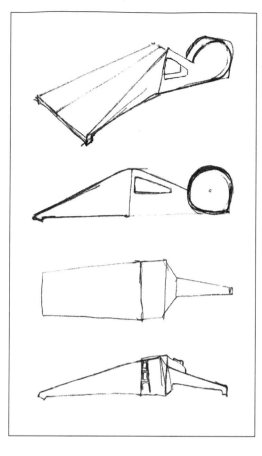

Don't draw only furniture. Use a sketchbook for recording lots of forms, including man-made shapes such as this battery-operated vacuum cleaner.

If you are drawing while sitting in an easy chair, the sketchbook can be inclined in your lap to get the proper orientation. If you are on a stool at a drawing table, tilt the surface so that your lines of sight are perpendicular to the page. If you are working at a flat desk, lean over the desk slightly or prop up the sketchbook. Some designers like to stand at a desk and look directly down at the sketchbook.

Some simple warm-up exercises before sketching will tune your hand-to-eye coordination, limber up your muscles, reduce "blank-page" anxiety and get you in the mood for sketching. Begin by drawing parallel lines, first vertically, then horizontally.

Leg lineup. *Sketches are useful for comparing ideas, such as the leg options (below) for the desk above.*

Keep them close together but not touching or overlapping. Try to make all the lines the same length, using quick, deliberate strokes. To gain confidence, start with short lines, then progress to longer ones, say, half the page length. Do 15 or 20, drawing from top to bottom and left to right, then reverse direction. The vertical and horizontal lines can be superimposed to form a grid, and you should strive to make the lines perpendicular.

Next, draw some 45° lines. These can be superimposed on the grid, if you like. Work from upper left to lower right, then reverse. Repeat, starting at the bottom of the page and drawing upward. Then move on to radi-

A design come to life. *Large freehand drawings, like the one at right, make an object look realistic.*

ating lines, starting each line at the center of an imaginary circle, drawing a radius and shifting each successive line about 5°. Try drawing from the center outward, then from the imaginary circumference inward, toward the center. Start working clockwise, then move counterclockwise.

Now try sketching concentric circles. Work from small to large, then from large to small; first clockwise, then counterclockwise. Similar exercises can be done with ovals, curved lines of various configurations and other geometric forms, such as triangles and octagons.

These warm-up exercises need take only five minutes. If you are new to sketching, I'd suggest doing these right in your sketchbook so that you have a record of your developing skills.

Some sketching techniques

When you start sketching, use the same long strokes you used in the warm-ups. Avoid short, choppy lines, which give drawings a hesitant, staccato-like quality. Instead, use long, single strokes, which look confident and result in more interesting and expressive sketches.

Resist the urge to use technical drawing aids, such as rulers, compasses, or circle and ellipse templates. Your goal should be to develop hand-to-eye coordination and free-hand drawing skills. As you progress, you will find your sketches becoming more expressive and personal.

Throw away your eraser, too—it is impossible to make a mistake in your sketchbook. If you draw a line that is not quite right, so be it. Simply redraw a second, third or fourth line over the original until it

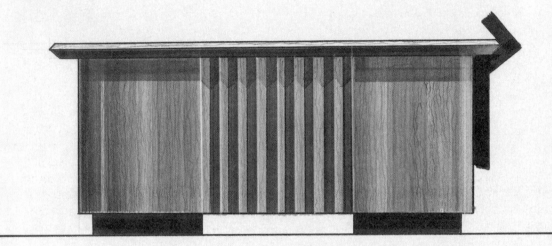

Sketches build on each other. *This desk went through a series of incarnations, two of which are shown here, before the author settled on the final design (opposite).*

looks right. Emphasize the correct line by making it darker or wider, or obscure rejected lines by working them into shading or a background shadow. Before you discard and redraw a line, however, examine it for what it may be suggesting. There are artists who will never redraw a line, but rather pursue what first comes out on the paper.

Always try to draw large, avoiding thumbnail sketches. The line width in these tiny drawings is often disproportionate to the rest of the image, and the size just does not allow for sufficient detail. Large warm-up exercises will encourage you to make bigger, bolder sketches that will be far more informative. Put several of these larger sketches on a single page, particularly if they represent a developing idea for the same piece of furniture.

As you design with your sketchbook, keep the pencil moving on the paper, spending as little time as possible sitting idle. Although you will inevitably form mental pictures of a piece, try to let these images come from the sketching, rather than imagining a piece first in your mind and then trying to draw it.

Looking and seeing

When designing a piece of furniture, try not to look only at furniture for inspiration. Look at paintings, sculpture, architecture and graphic design. Observe nature, too—rock formations, tree structure, leaves and flowers. Manufactured objects, particularly after they have degenerated and been discarded, are rich with forms to stimulate the imagination.

If you do look at furniture, look at lots of it. Look at so much that you can't remember the details of any single piece. What you will retain are concepts, feelings and generalities that are fertile for design development. When fishing for inspiration, cast a wide net. Use your sketchbook as a camera to record ideas for future development.

Finally, never throw out a sketch. When you see old sketches, perhaps years after they were drawn, you will have had a tremendous number of visual experiences. You will see the old drawings through a different set of eyes, and invariably you will notice something that you missed the first time. Your sketchbooks will become a renewable resource for inspiration.

FROM CONCEPT TO CABINET

by John Gallagher

The idea came easily. I wanted to build a china cabinet that would hold dishes for a small family. It would have a glass upper case, where delicate glass and china could be displayed, and underneath I envisioned drawers, several shelves for silverware, plates and other items. I wanted to avoid something too great in size, thinking that it should be big enough to hold a dinner set for a family but not wind up as a catch-all for unused items.

But even with the function and general proportions of the cabinet clearly understood, its character was not. The question was how to get from the glimmerings of an idea to a fully developed plan. A few years ago, I might have done a few drawings and then gone directly into the construction—not because I was more confident but because I was less well-equipped to steer the design process.

Recently, while I was a student at the College of the Redwoods in Fort Bragg, California, James Krenov taught me how to use sketches, models and mockups to give definite shape to my ideas. Drawings get initial ideas recorded so that they can be seen and considered. Scale models and full-size mockups give physical presence to the drawings, letting me see a piece in detail before I've cut the first piece of wood.

With this approach, which utilizes construction skills during the design process, the search for form begins to blend with the craft of woodworking, making a seamless flow from the first notion to the finished cabinet. More of the senses come into play. Perceptions of depth and volume are tapped as well as gut feelings about how a piece relates to human scale. Before a piece is even built, you can see the way light and shadow will play on its surfaces. And the sense of touch—so critical to the experience of using furniture—is involved during the design stage instead of having to wait until the building begins. Using more of your senses early on makes a richer, more intimate experience for the imagination to work with.

This design process of using sketches, models and mockups isn't necessarily a straight line, and there is no one correct way to use the tools involved. For those uncomfortable with drawing, it provides other means to develop ideas. For those who like to draw, it is a way to translate drawings into three dimensions. The three tools can be used together or in any combination. In designing my china cabinet, I used all of them but not in the order I had anticipated.

Sketching exploration

To explore the general idea for my piece, I sketched various versions in front view, adding side and perspective drawings when I found one that was particularly attractive. I was looking to draw a cabinet with a balanced, grounded feel and with a bit of grace in its stance to avoid heaviness. Using light pencil pressure, I roughed in the general proportions of the cabinet and then returned to darken the best lines. To some drawings I

added shading, grain or color. In this type of drawing, I'm not trying for perfect results. Wavy lines are fine for sampling ideas and can even have a charm of their own.

Sometimes a couple of sketches are enough to catch the general feel of the original idea; sometimes, a couple of dozen. I made several sketches that were close to what I had in mind (drawings below). My sketches showed a closed lower case with a light framework to hold the glass in the upper part of the cabinet. I opted for a frame-and-panel back to add visual interest. The lower doors and sides were plain. The cabinet front was bowed, which increased storage space yet did not add much to overall size. It had a simple stand beneath.

Exploring on paper _____

In his early drawings for a piece of furniture, the author plays with proportion, making loose sketches of a range of possibilities. Then he selects one or two sketches to render more carefully.

Model sprung from a sketch. The author's models are fleshed-out sketches. When he has a sketch he likes, he makes the model by taking dimensions directly from the sketch.

I disregard scale while sketching because I'm really searching for proportion and form, not exact dimensions. Scale is an unnecessary taskmaster at this point and can be worked out after a good drawing has been made.

From sketch to mockup

I made a drawing I liked and decided to make a mockup from it. To establish the dimensions of the cabinet, I made a paper scale. I placed a ½-inch wide strip of paper on the sketch and made a mark on the strip at the top and bottom of the drawing. Because I wanted the cabinet to be 60 inches tall, I divided the distance between the marks into 60 equal units. Once I had determined the length of an inch at this scale, I measured the other dimensions with the paper strip.

When the mockup was finished (see photo pp. 14-15), I saw that the drawer-to-molding transition was too wide, robbing height from the already short lower half of the cabinet. I felt the cabinet needed a course correction. In this case, the mockup had told me what I did not want but not what I did want.

Not long after building the mockup, while talking to a friend about the project, I made a quick sketch on a chalkboard to illustrate a point. I realized I had caught something I liked. The proportions were unusual but seemed to fit. I copied it in my sketchbook to save the idea. It was similar

to the first drawing but with a shift in proportions. I moved the drawers to the inside of the cabinet, which gave more height to the lower doors, and I shortened the glass case to about half the height of the lower case. My cabinet grew out of that sketch.

Make your mistakes before you make your furniture. Models allow you to try new ideas without a great commitment of time or money.

This cabinet's elegance is no accident. The author worked through a series of versions of his olive-ash china cabinet on paper, in mock-ups and in a model before he began building the real thing.

Model springs from a sketch

Not wanting to commit to another mockup immediately after making my new drawing, I instead built a model. I made it in a few hours. I bandsawed the cabinet's case out of solid wood. To represent the glass and the framework in the upper cabinet, I glued thin wooden strips over white paper. I cut out miniature feet with a knife and glued them in place. I built the model by measuring right off my sketch (see top photo p. 17).

After seeing the problems revealed by the mockup, I wanted to be sure that the new version of my cabinet wouldn't look top-heavy. I was also concerned that with four legs in the base, the bowed front might appear unsupported. The model assured me that the new proportions of the upper and lower cases were right—about one-third above and two-thirds below—and that the cabinet would have a balanced stance.

Models are fun to make, take little time and use virtually no materials. They help me visualize the final results from any perspective, even from above. I'll often set one on the bench or windowsill while I continue with other matters. Having the model in the shop keeps the design process alive, and good ideas come along even when I'm not actively seeking them.

A mockup is a 3-D sketch

Models and mockups serve different purposes. Both allow you to see an object in the round, but mockups, being full-size, give a better sense of volume and of the relationship to human proportion. Details can be mocked up individually or as parts of the whole before any expensive wood is laid on a sawhorse. I often make mockups by assembling components, so ideas can easily be altered and refined (right photo, opposite page).

I had about a day in making the original mockup. Because I had used drywall screws for assembly, it took only another few hours to modify it for its reincarnation. I used dry 2x4s and 1/8-inch plywood for ease of construction and economy. I bandsawed the legs and frame parts out of the 2x4s and used the plywood for the lower portion of the cabinet.

Mockups are made to be manipulated. The author uses dark masking tape to "erase" wood on the feet and the crown molding. A quick pass with a pencil simulates grain. Pine mullions are press-fit in the upper doors. The mockup is made as a stack of components, so it is easy to modify.

Modifying a mockup

I liked the overall lines and proportions of my revised mockup as much as I had liked the model and the sketch. But some of the details were bothersome. The legs in the mockup stand were too heavy and so was the glass frame and the top of the cabinet. I thinned them down visually with dark masking tape instead of disassembling the mockup and cutting. I applied tape to the legs and penciled the new shape on the tape. Then I scored the pencil line with a sharp knife and peeled the tape off along one side of the line. The tape that remained obscured part of the leg, making it look thinner. The same effect can be achieved by scribbling with a dark pencil. I also used tape to thin the top (left photo, above).

I worked on the molded edges in the transition between upper and lower parts of the cabinet in the mockup. I wanted a clear delineation, but I didn't want it to be too elaborate. Still, I wound up doing some fine-tuning on the actual cabinet. By milling a small cove, I created a shadowline and gave some variation for the eyes to rest on (photo, facing page).

Sometimes I tape butcher paper to the front of a mocked-up cabinet and draw various treatments on the paper. I might draw frame-and-panel doors on one sheet, then tape another sheet over the first and draw doors like the ones on my china cabinet. On a bureau I might sketch a bank of five drawers, then overlay another drawing showing it with seven. The butcher paper lets you play with different grain patterns as well.

For this cabinet, I had planned to cut a plank of olive ash into veneers. The wood had a distinct difference between its darker heartwood and pale sapwood, and I wanted to include both. I spring-clamped the veneer around the lower case of the mockup in a variety of combinations. I tried slip-matching them, but the resulting stripes were too busy. When I bookmatched the veneers with the sapwood in the center, they gave the cabinet a feeling of repose. I clipped veneer to each side with a vertical band of sapwood at the back, providing some continuity with the front.

I cut mullions for the mockup so that I could press-fit them in the upper doors. This way I could experiment with different placements of the mullions in the doors. I also experimented with the cabinet's curved front. The bow is not an arc of a circle; the curve tightens as it approaches the sides. I had to play with the curve to get one I liked, and the mockup allowed me to do that easily.

Clay makes quick pulls. A lump of modeling clay and five minutes of manipulation were all it took to see what the cabinet would look like with handles.

Shop drawings from the mockup

When I was satisfied with the mockup, I developed working drawings directly from it. I made a top-view drawing of the upper and lower halves of the cabinet, showing the placement of the dowels, rabbets for the back panels and the thickness of the doors and the glued-on edges. This view also provided me with the exact shape for the curved bending forms for the veneered doors below and the bent-laminated doors above.

Overall, I find it helpful and appropriate that the scale and the mechanical drawings are introduced only after the character of the piece is established. They are kept where they should be: in a supporting role.

Use of mockups and models as well as drawings makes designing a piece of furniture a much more absorbing and reliable process. For me, even the wrong turns and false starts reaffirm the value of this approach to design. It lets me set a course for arriving at a design and lets me assess its merit and make adjustments along the way. This is the best of both worlds: exploring ideas while preserving possibilities.

Molding marks the transition from lower case to upper. The small cove along the top of the lower piece of molding creates a shadowline and provides a curved place for the eye to rest. It delineates the two parts of the cabinet without dividing them.

TWO

Organizing Your Projects

Every year, commercial plans, cut lists, and step-by-step instructions help millions of woodworkers make furniture. They take the confusion out of the process by delivering answers for almost every conceivable question that might come up, from the exact dimensions of every piece to the order in which they should be made and assembled. For beginning woodworkers, these plans are essential when building large, complex pieces. For that matter, plans are useful to all types of woodworker the first time they build a particular piece.

However, for the same reason woodworkers make furniture instead of buying it, many also make their own plans and cut lists. Commercial plans and step-by-step instructions lock you into someone else's ways of thinking and working. The recommended tools might not be the ones in your shop. And when you're making your own furniture, the projects don't come with plans.

Developing an idea for a piece of furniture on a sketch pad and carrying it through is a fairly simple process, but not without its pitfalls. Visualizing the final piece before committing wood to the table saw is crucial. This is hard to do in your mind, so Jan Zaitlin recommends making a model. Models sort out all the aspects of a design that a sketch can't and offer a very real-looking representation of the finished piece. Zaitlin's models are quick and cheap to make, so they're a wise investment at this stage in the game.

Once the design is finalized, every project needs a plan of execution. Jim Tolpin and Ed Speas run through the strategies they use to keep large projects under control. Their tools are simple but effective: drawings, a bill of materials, cut lists, and good layout tools. Efficient and organized woodworking is good woodworking. It prevents mistakes, saving time and materials. It also saves aggravation, making the work that much more enjoyable.

MODELS SOLVE DESIGN AND CONSTRUCTION PROBLEMS

by Jan Zaitlin

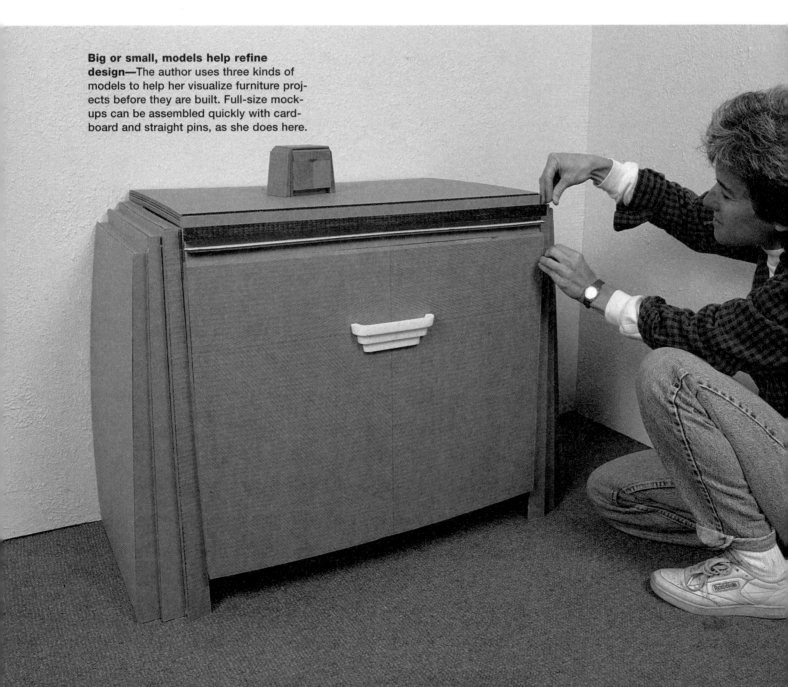

Big or small, models help refine design—The author uses three kinds of models to help her visualize furniture projects before they are built. Full-size mock-ups can be assembled quickly with cardboard and straight pins, as she does here.

I'm a big fan of making models and mock-ups before I move on to a finished piece of furniture. Whether the prototypes are cardboard or foam, full size or one-eighth scale, they help solve a long list of furnituremaking problems. Models are good for demonstrating knockdown features and can help me decide what construction techniques to use. Clients love models because visualizing the real thing from drawings can be difficult; models can show clients how finished pieces will look in their intended room settings. Even if I'm building a project for myself, a quick model can prevent disappointments later.

I use several types of models, and the applications and the materials for each vary. I have three favorites: the quick, full-scale mock-up, what I call the scale appearance model, and the full-size detail mock-up like the one in the photo above.

A quick, full-scale mock-up

A mock-up is a quick, inexpensive, full-scale, approximation of the completed piece. The purpose is to catch any obvious mistakes in proportion. I usually build one right after I have my design concept drawn, dimensioned and approved. The mock-up shouldn't take more than an hour to construct and should be taken to the site. There, I can tell if the finished piece will be the right size for the intended space, if it blocks too much light or if its position or dimensions will cause some other unexpected problem, such as limiting the swing of a door. If the project is a dining table, I can place chairs around the mock-up to see if it makes the room seem too crowded, allows room for serving platters and seats the required number of people comfortably.

I use inexpensive materials that can be worked quickly. Mock-ups need not be pretty. For most projects, I use corrugated cardboard, which can be used for curved as well as angular projects because I can bend it with the "grain." And I can draw on it with a pencil or marker to suggest details.

Sometimes the appropriate mock-up material is foam board, polystyrene foam sandwiched between smooth paper. Foam board looks cleaner than cardboard, and it doesn't have the strong grain that corrugated

cardboard has. It is available at art and architectural supply stores and comes in a range of thicknesses ($1/8$ in., $3/16$ in., $1/2$ in.) and in sheet sizes up to 4 ft. by 8 ft.

Both foam board and cardboard are easily cut with a utility knife. I use a cordless hot-melt glue gun for quick assembly. On those occasions where hot-melt glue is not appropriate (it can be messy and thick), I have used a quick-drying white glue called Elmer's Tacky Glue. I also use a variety of tapes including repositionable tape, which is good for changing things around. Check the adhesives section in art- or graphic-supply stores.

A handy fastener for butt joining is an ordinary straight pin, the kind used by tailors to hold fabric together. These are available at fabric stores and often at grocery and drug stores. Straight pins are great for making a knockdown mock-up (see the photo on the facing page).

For more sculptural applications, such as a chair or lamp base, or wherever it is important to show mass, I use rigid blue foam (extruded polystyrene). It is used in construction as insulation and comes in 2-ft. by 8-ft. sheets, 1 in. and 2 in. thick. Avoid the white foam. It breaks up into little pellets and doesn't sand well. 3M makes a spray adhesive especially for foam that bonds almost instantly, so you can stack up layers of foam to get a mass of material very quickly.

Cushion that's really foam—High-density, white polyurethane foam shapes easily and is perfect to mimic upholstery in scale models.

Zion-Benton Public Library District

Simple fixture makes cutting small model parts safer—The author made a small crosscut fixture for her radial-arm saw to reduce the danger of small parts getting pushed through the big gap in a standard saw fence.

Blue foam can be worked quickly with most woodworking machinery and hand tools. The board can cut cleanly with both a bandsaw and a tablesaw, sanded quickly with a disc sander (be sure to use a dust mask) or sculpted with a Surform tool or a file (see the photo on p. 25).

Other materials are also useful for mock-ups: scrap wood for those times when cardboard just isn't strong enough, aluminum foil to simulate a mirror or metal parts and construction paper or poster board bent, cut or used like a veneer. Be creative.

When you build your mock-up, it's a good idea to make it easy to alter, so you can make changes without too much trouble. After all, you're really trying to see how the shape and proportion work, so a mock-up that's easy to adjust will be a lot more helpful than one with permanent joints. Be sure it is easy to disassemble, so the mock-up can be moved to a site or stored until completion of the real piece. Don't be tempted to toss the mock-up before the piece is completed. It will come in handy when you need to try out design changes that occur in mid-project.

A scale appearance model

After the mock-up, I consider making an appearance model—a scale model that looks like the real piece only smaller. I make appearance models when I am designing a piece for production or if a one-of-a-kind piece is particularly sculptural, uses unusual construction techniques or if the concept cannot be conveyed adequately with a drawing. A model gives a more realistic sense of the finished piece, especially if your drawing skills are weak; it makes a great presentation tool, and it can be used to create photos of a room setting when the job site isn't available for a mock-up. A nice appearance model takes a day or two to build.

I make appearance models of furniture at one-eighth or one-quarter scale, according to the size of the project. It's best not to go overboard on detail, or the model begins to look too cute, like doll furniture. Small details also take time to do well and often don't tell you much. If they are really important, do the third type of model, a full-scale detail mock-up. More on that later.

Wood is the primary material on most of my appearance models. I used to mill my own small stock, but I found that it was time-consuming to cut the very thin stock that is necessary. And quite often, the quality was not as good as the store-bought model-making material. It can be tricky to mill small stock without having it explode in the planer or chip badly. Many hobby shops and architectural supply stores carry a good selection of basswood, cherry and walnut. I avoid balsa because it doesn't cut cleanly. Many of the places that carry model-making supplies also sell ultra-thin plywood. I have seen three-layer sheets (1 ft. by 2 ft.) of ply as thin as $1/64$ in.

When the project calls for a substance other than wood, I use a variety of materials. The blue foam mentioned earlier is good for simulating the pleats, folds and soft look of upholstery. There is a better quality, white, high-density polyurethane foam available in sheets $1/4$ in. to 2 in. thick that is more expensive but holds details better and is more uniform (see the photo on p. 25). You can paint it with acrylic paint.

Acrylic sheet or rod can be used to simulate metal or glass. It can be bent with heat from a heat gun, torch or in an oven and painted with a metallic paint. I have used pieces of acrylic sheet to simulate glass tabletops by painting the edges green (a light green marker is even easier).

Painted wood used to offend the woodworking purist in me. But now I see that it can be used to simulate other materials. For example, there are faux marble paint kits available in paint stores or art supply stores, so you can machine a tabletop in wood and then make it look like marble or granite. To make the patterns look right on scale models, you may have to alter your technique slightly. For instance, to get a smaller pattern that looks right, a tight-pored sponge, like a sea sponge, works best for marbling.

Don't overlook paper as a model-making material. When used like a veneer, it is quicker than paint and can simulate laminates and stone. Art or graphic supply stores carry paper in glossy or matte finishes, and the number of colors will surprise you. Ask for Pantone paper. While you are in the graphics department, get a can of instant spray adhesive made just for paper.

And don't leave until you check out some markers, pencils and press-on stripes and patterns. Architects and designers use these to simulate details; you can too. You can draw on inlays or drawer and door lines. A dot can simulate a knob, a horizontal line can suggest a wire pull and markers can simulate aniline dyes. There are wood-colored markers, but you need to test the color to see if it approximates the real wood color.

Special tools help model making

Though the construction of scale models can be relatively quick, it requires some special tools and fixtures to make the machining of small parts safe and accurate. For example, I made a small-parts crosscut jig for my radial-arm saw (see the photo on the facing page). The jig helps block off the big gap in the fence that could swallow up small parts as they are being cut to length.

To deal with this gap problem on the tablesaw, I made a wooden throat plate with a narrow slot. I also can rip thin material on the tablesaw without having it slip under the bottom edge of the fence by using an easily installed facing for the fence that goes all the way down to the table surface. I always use push sticks; sometimes I use two, one in each hand. Featherboards are also good for keeping your fingers away from the cutting edges.

Joinery for models

I often simplify the joinery on appearance models. I use butt joints when I can get away with it, but I also use thin dowels or wooden toothpicks for through-dowel joints when necessary. Dado joints are pretty easy with a router table and $1/16$-in. and $1/8$-in. straight bits. Make certain that the hole in the table is not so large that it creates a safety hazard when machining small parts. I use little De-Sta-Co clamps to make quick jigs to hold the small parts when I machine them on the router table.

Mortise-and-tenon joinery may seem a bit extreme, but occasionally, I find that it provides detailing important to the look of the finished piece. And it may help hold the model together. I drill out holes and clean out corners just like I do in full-scale mortise joints, but I use a shopmade $1/16$-in. chisel. I made the chisel by grinding the tang end of an old, dull file. The steel is hard enough to keep an edge.

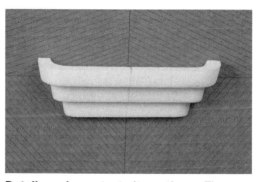

Detail mock-ups test alternatives—The author used white foam to make a full-size detail mock-up of a cabinet handle. Several options can be made as detail mock-ups and then tried out on the quick, full-size mock-up.

Photos make models look real

Models let you look at the result in advance. This scale model of a conference table comes to life when photographed with a few props and an appropriate background. Cardboard or clear acrylic human figures add scale.

Scale models that are made with care can be photographed to look like full-size pieces, as shown above. This is a great design and presentation tool.

Determine the background

The easiest background is a sheet of paper large enough to fill the picture frame. Use any color paper as long as it isn't glossy. Bend the paper, don't crease it, so it sits on a tabletop and runs up a wall behind the table. For a more dramatic effect, use a roll of background paper, available in a variety of colors from professional photo supply stores. Tack one end to the wall, and put a table about 3 ft. away from the wall. Roll the paper onto the table, and set the roll on the floor. Place the model on the paper near the front of the table, and

focus light there. The background fades into darkness, which contrasts with the lighted model.

Photos of the piece on site

To see what the piece will look like on site, I use three pieces of foam board taped together on the back side to form two walls and a floor large enough to house the model and fill the picture frame (see the photo on the facing page). To give a sense of scale, I use a few props. This can be as simple to do as drawing an outline of a door with a circle for a knob at the right height. When I was photographing a model of an audio-visual storage system, I drew a screen on a cardboard television set, which was just a rectangle of gray cardboard propped up from behind with a little cardboard triangle.

Figures add human dimension

I find scale figures helpful, too. You can make a quick one by photocopying a figure from an architectural graphics book or a department store advertisement. Enlarge or reduce the figure until it is the right size. Use spray mount to fix the figure as a cutting guide to any rigid, thin material, like ⅛-in. acrylic. Then glue a small triangle to the back of the figure to make it stand on its own.

Photo tips

In addition to a 35mm camera, I would suggest that you use a macro lens or a set of magnifying lenses, called close-up filters, which screw onto a lens to allow you to focus at much closer distances than standard lenses. A tripod and a cable shutter release allow you to snap a shot without wiggling the camera. Light stands can be fashioned with clamp-on shop lights and a chair for a stand. But daylight shooting is often quicker and can be just as effective. Just be sure that your film is matched to whatever lighting you choose. Any good photo supply store can give you advice on choosing the correct film.

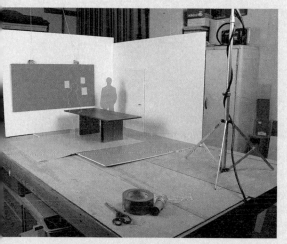

Three pieces of foam board can make a room—With the camera pulled back, the illusion is revealed. The backdrop is held up by string and tape. Simple shop-style clamp lights can substitute for the electronic flash shown here.

One store-bought model-making tool that I find useful is the tiny brass bar clamp. I got a pair of them as a gift and thought I would never use them, but the bar clamps are handy because they fit in small places. Other good clamping tools are clothespins, paper clips, tape and rubber bands.

Scaled construction hints at real problems

Although the tools are smaller, scale model making provides a good opportunity to think through the whole construction process on full-scale pieces. As I build the model, I imagine that I am doing everything in full scale, and based on that experience, I choose the best construction technique for the real piece. It is important to remember that if a construction operation or detail is easy in scale, it may not be when it is full size and vice versa. For example, once I neglected to account for how difficult it would be to lift a glass top in and out of a frame repeatedly to get a perfect fit; on the model, it was easy to fit because the small piece of acrylic was light. Conversely, some things can be awkward on a scale model because the access is tight or the parts are so small that clamping is difficult, but on the real thing, access may be a matter of reaching your arm inside a cabinet or using a bar clamp.

Full-scale detail mock-up

Mies van der Rohe, the famous architect, once said, "God is in the details." So when I am working on a piece that has unusual edge or surface treatment, a unique pull, connection or foot, I mock up just the detail. The full-scale detail mock-up lets you see your design in three dimensions. If you have already made a full-scale mock-up of the entire piece, then it's a good idea to attach this detail mock-up to it (see the photo on p. 27). Work precisely on the detail mock-up so that you can work from it to build the real thing.

My material of choice is foam, both the blue and white types discussed earlier, because foam is so easy to work. When I use wood, I prefer something that can be worked easily, such as pine. Wood is the obvious choice if the detail is turned on the lathe or if it requires a texture that cannot be expressed in some other quickly worked material.

ORGANIZE YOUR PROJECTS

by Jim Tolpin

Once you have a clear vision of a woodworking project, either through concept sketches or from measuring an existing piece, the next step is to create a bridge between the idea and the actual construction. This means defining your vision on paper with working drawings, usually a three-view (orthographic) projection.

I use these drawings to generate a bill of materials, which functions both as an order sheet and as a data base from which to develop the cutting lists—one for solid stock and one for sheet stock, if any. These lists show the number, the size and the detailing of every piece of wood that goes into the project. Sometimes I also make graphic representations of the cutting lists to help me determine the most efficient use of the stock (see the photo on the facing page). Last, I cross-check carefully from the drawing to the bill of materials to the cutting lists to make sure that they all agree.

Once you have accurate cutting lists in hand, you can begin the actual construction process by laying out the components. When all the parts are marked on the stock, it's clear sailing—no more knitted brow and clenched teeth. You can leave behind all that left-brain, analytical thinking and enjoy the process of cutting, shaping and assembling the components.

Creating a bill of materials

To ensure that all the parts of a project will be accounted for in the bill of materials, and later in the cutting lists, create a referencing system. On the three-view drawing, label each component with a circled letter. You needn't bother to label separate identical components, such as four legs of an end table (as long as they're all made from the same material). To make organizing the bill saner, especially with large, complex projects, label the largest components first, working your way down to details such as moldings and drawer parts. Be sure to place material under the appropriate stock heading—solid or sheet—and add a notation for species if you're using more than one kind of wood.

As you list each item in the bill of materials, add a second circle around the letter on the drawing. When all the letters are double-circled, you'll have accounted for every component. Double-check by comparing the number of items on your bill of materials against a count of components shown in the drawing.

When listing widths and lengths of components on the bill of materials, be sure you've taken any joinery into account. It's easy to overlook the extra length you'll need for tenons or the width for tongues when joining boards with tongues and grooves. If your three-view drawing does not specify the sizes of these joints, lay them out on a full-scale drawing. Unless you note otherwise, assume that the length of the components runs with the grain of the wood.

Bill of materials to cutting lists

Develop the cutting lists directly from the bill of materials, collating the components by function and then by dimension. Establish a heading for thickness first, and then create subsidiary columns for each width (see the photo above). Under the appropriate width, write in the length of each piece. If the components aren't simply square-sided (without profile), add a cross-sectional graphic next to the length. If there are a number of identical parts, make tick marks to the right of the length to indicate how many. Don't confuse yourself with numerals here. As with the bill of materials, list the largest pieces first, double-circle the

letter symbol on the bill once you transfer it to the cutting list and double-check by comparing the number of components on your bill of materials and cutting list.

If I have a lot of components to cut out of sheet stock, I make a graphic cutting diagram (scaled drawings of 4x8 panels) on which I juggle the layout of the components to get the most out of each sheet. I account for sawkerfs, and I pay attention to grain by book-matching pairs of doors or cutting a bank of drawer faces from a single section of a sheet, for example. To make the panels easier to handle, I try to arrange the components so that the first cuts are full-length rips, giving me lighter stock to deal with when crosscutting.

From three-view drawing to bill of materials to cutting list, step-by-step organization can all but eliminate measurement errors. By taking care of the calculations and accounting up front, you can concentrate on attaining accuracy and perfecting technique.

Laying out on solid stock

With the cutting lists completed and double-checked against the bill of materials, you're ready to lay out the components on the boards. As you bring each previously thicknessed board to a leveled pair of sawhorses, set them down so that most defects face up. Mark the locations of any defects from the underside of the board onto the visible face with chalk. Always "waste" a minimum of an inch at each end of a board when squaring it, and take off more if splits are obvious.

If the board rocks on the leveled sawhorses or bows significantly, it's probably best used for short components. Try to lay out components to make the most efficient use of a board. Work around knots and other defects, keeping an eye out for grain matches and striving for an overall pleasing look for the visible faces of a project. Finally, try to arrange the layout so the offcuts are long lengths; shorter, wider offcut pieces generally make less useful stock for future projects.

Use a piece of chalk or a timber crayon to mark out the pieces on the stock. Lay out pieces $1/2$ in. long at this point and at least $3/16$ in. wide. It's easier to remove wood later than it is to add it back. Leave pieces even wider if you know the stock tends to curve as it's ripped. As you locate each component on the boards, pencil in a tick mark to the left of the length notation on the cutting list. When the tick marks on the left equal those on the right, all the pieces of this width and length have been accounted for.

Laying out sheet stock

Panels are a lot easier to lay out than boards. Stock sizes are uniform, edges are straight, and except for occasional shipping damage, defects are negligible. If you're going to cut panels on a tablesaw and your rip fence and crosscut box are accurate and reliable, there's no need to transfer the layout from the graphic cutting diagram to the stock. Simply set the rip fence or stop on the crosscut box to the measurements on the cutting list, and make the cuts. Label each component along an edge with a marking pen, and put a second circle around the symbol denoting that component on the cutting diagram.

Joinery and complex shapes

Once you've cut out all the components, it's time to lay out for joinery, assembly positions and for any shaped (non-rectilinear) components. I don't use measurements to do this, though, because for me, placing my faith in numbers at this stage is an invitation to disaster. Instead, I use a full-scale drawing. Then I either transfer it directly to my stock using a pounce wheel, a small, gear-like wheel designed for this purpose (see the photo on the facing page) or I make a template. When using the pounce wheel, I fol-

Drawing an arc

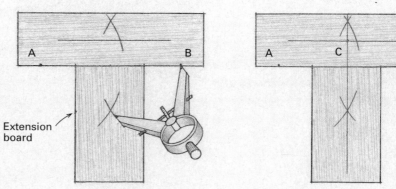

Workpiece

Height of arc

A   B

1) Mark points A and B, where the arc leaves the stock, and draw a line indicating the height of the arc.

2) Swing compass or trammel from points A and B, both above the height of the arc and below the stock, on an extension board.

A   B

Extension board

3) Draw a line through the points defined by the intersection of the compass or trammel beam swings. Point C is the apex of the arc.

A   C   B

A pounce wheel is useful for transferring layout information either directly to the stock, if you only want one piece of that design, or onto template material, such as ⅛-in. lauan plywood or Masonite, if you want a more permanent record to reproduce the piece later.

low the wheel with a light chalk dusting or with a pencil line to make the impressions left by the wheel more visible. If there's a chance I'll want to make a piece again, I make a template; if I know a piece is a one-off, I just pounce onto the stock.

To transfer the shape of a complex or irregularly shaped component, such as a scalloped table apron, I always use a full-scale template. To make the template, I tape vellum tracing paper (available at art-supply stores) over the area of the full-scale drawing containing the component and trace its shape with a #2½ pencil. Then I pounce the pattern onto a piece of ⅛-in. lauan plywood. I bandsaw this pattern to within 1/16 in. of the line, and then use rasps, files and sandpaper to finish the job. I can use this plywood pattern to reproduce the component indefinitely. A set of templates representing each component contains all the

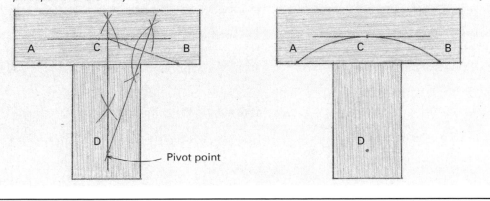

4) Repeat steps 2 and 3, except swing from B and C instead of A and B. Where this new line (perpendicular to the segment between D and C) intersects the line you drew in step 3 is the pivot point for the arc you wish to draw.

5) Set compass or trammel to the distance between D and A (or B). Swing arc through A, B and C.

Pivot point

information I need to reproduce a project; it's a durable, accurate and highly efficient way to keep this information at hand.

Laying out a curve with a batten

To draw a fair curve, whether on a full-scale drawing, a template or directly on the stock, use a batten held to a series of points along the curve (see the photo below). I make battens from clear, close-grained wood. Old-growth fir or spruce is ideal, though nearly any knot-free, straight-grained stock will do. Cut the batten square to keep the curve fair—from 1/8 in. for tight bends to 3/4 in. for long, gentle curves.

To determine a few points along the curve, draw a 1-in. grid pattern over the area of the full-scale drawing containing the curve. Draw the grid on actual stock or on template stock. Determine where the curve intersects the grid lines on the drawing, and transfer those points to the grid on the wood. When working from a scaled drawing, draw the grid on the drawing at the same scale, lay out the curve at scale and transfer it to the wood.

Bending a batten to points along a curve is the best way to lay out long, gentle curves. For fair curves, use a square batten.

Set finish nails at those points, and bend the batten stock to touch each nail. Prevent the stick from breaking by applying the bending force from near the end of the batten rather than just beyond the points you've marked. Where necessary, sandwich the stick between two nails to hold it in place. At the ends of the curve where the batten leaves the board, add extension boards to which you can fasten the free ends of the batten. Don't let the protruding ends just run straight. That would cause the curve on the board to go out of fair between the points marked on the stock.

Before drawing in the curve, eyeball it. You can readily see if it's a sweet, fair curve. Don't hesitate to let your eye overrule a marked point to make it fair.

Drawing an arc with a compass

If a curve is nothing more than an arc (a portion of a circle), you can use a compass or a trammel beam to draw it. The only trick is finding the center of the circle—the pivot point for the compass or the beam. It's not difficult to do, but it's not exactly intuitive either, hearkening back to high-school geometry, which may not be all that fresh in your mind anymore. The drawing on pp. 32-33 shows you how.

Laying out rounded corners

Unofficially, I draw in rounded corners by reaching into my pocket, taking out a fistful of change and using a coin as a round template: A penny produces a 3/8-in. radius arc; a quarter produces about a 1/2-in. arc and a half dollar gives you a 5/8-in. arc. For larger radii, I've even rummaged through my finish supplies for cans with a radius close to what I wanted.

Officially, and when I'm out of change or fed up with using out-of-round cans that leave a ring of old paint or oil on the wood, I use a marking gauge and compass to draw in a rounded corner quickly and accurately (see the near right photo). I set the marking gauge to the radius I desire and run the gauge along each edge of the wood to the corner. At the intersection of the lines, I place the pivot point of my compass, which

Laying out round corners is easy with marking gauge and compass. Set both for the same radius, mark intersecting lines with the gauge, and you have a pivot point.

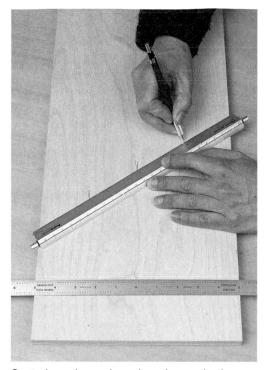

Centering rules and regular rules are both useful for locating centers. They can also be used for establishing regular intervals across a board's width.

I've set to the same radius as the marking gauge, and I draw in the rounded corner.

Laying out equal divisions

Sometimes, when laying out a piece of furniture, you need to divide a board into parts of equal width, whether halves, thirds or more parts. Centerlines are often needed to locate joint cut lines or assembly positions. Multiple divisions are needed to locate the parts of certain joints, such as dovetails. Components that are to be located evenly between two points, such as chair slats, must be laid out so they end up with equal spacings between them. The process can seem complicated, but with certain layout tools and just a little bit of arithmetic (the first and only time I'll burden you with number crunching), these tasks can be made a lot easier.

The simplest way to find a centerline across the width of a board is to use a centering rule, a rule that reads both to the right and to the left of a 0 at the center of the straightedge (see the photo above left).

To find a center point, you need only position the rule so that the same number appears over each edge, and the 0 will indicate the center point.

A standard rule can be used to locate any number of equal divisions across a width. Let's say that you want to divide an 11-in. board into four equal pieces. To do this, lay the rule on the board with the 0 point over an edge. Then set the 12 (a multiple of 4) on the other edge of the board (see the photo above right). In most cases, you'll have to angle the rule to do this. Now just mark your division lines (here, 3, 6 and 9), and then extend or transfer them, using a marking gauge (or a combination square if the end of your board is square).

To draw centerlines over the length of a piece of stock, I made a simple centering marking gauge, consisting of two dowels, a little block of scrap and a common drywall screw (see the photo on p. 36). When using the gauge, it's important to keep the dowels tightly against both sides of the stock. A nice feature of this type of gauge is that the

An effective and cheap centering scribe can be made from a piece of scrapwood, two dowels and a drywall screw, as the author demonstrates above.

centerline remains true even if the stock changes in width along its length.

Now for the math. To determine the centerlines of a number of components spaced evenly between two points, it's necessary to know how many components you want to fit in the space and how wide the space is. Let's assume you want to space three chair slats evenly between chair posts that are $16^{1}/_{2}$ in. apart (see the drawing below). Add the width of one of the slats ($3^{1}/_{2}$ in. in this case) to the width of the space between the posts ($16^{1}/_{2}$ in.) for a total of 20 in., and then divide this sum by the total number of spaces (4) between slats and posts: 20 in./4 = 5 in. Now mark the centerlines of the outside slats at 5 in. less half the width of a slat ($1^{3}/_{4}$ in.), or $3^{1}/_{4}$ in. from the post. Mark the centerline of the middle slat at 5 in. from the centerlines of the two outside slats.

Spacing components evenly between two points

If components are centered on equal division lines, spacing won't be equal.

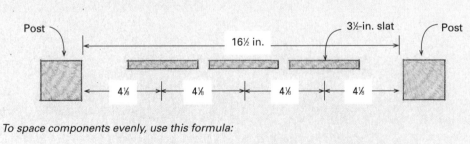

To space components evenly, use this formula:

S (spacing between components) = $\dfrac{\text{D (distance between posts)} + \text{W (width of slat)}}{\text{N (number of spaces between slats and posts)}}$

S = 16½ + 3½/4 = 5
S = 5 in.

Spacing between posts and outermost slats (end spacing, or ES) is determined by subtracting half the width of one slat from the spacing determined with the above formula.

ES = 5 − (½ x 3½)
ES = 3¼ in.

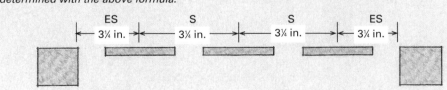

A project plan to keep things straight

by Ed Speas

Amateurs sometimes resist structure in their wood-working, thinking, "It's my hobby, my relaxation, my fun." But there's nothing relaxing about making mistakes and nothing fun about building ugly furniture. I was taught to build furniture following a specific procedure. Since learning and following this procedure, my furniture has been nicer looking and better built. Moreover, the process itself is more enjoyable now. Don't let the structure of this procedure scare you off. It's not meant to dictate every move you make or steal the enjoyment out of your work but rather to turn chaos into some type of order. Here's what I do:

1. Design: You need a design, whether your own or someone else's. Don't be afraid to sketch it out—you don't have to be an artist. Just get something on paper, so you can see the design rather than just imagining it.

2. Working drawings: These are simply ortho-graphic line drawings, which include front and side views, an overhead view and any sectional drawings needed. Now is when you start to assign dimensions to each part. These drawings don't need to be pretty; they just need to be accurate. A full-sized working drawing is best because it's easiest to judge proportions from, and you can also use it to determine angles and tapers for machine setups.

3. Mock-ups and models: This is a step that everyone should follow though few do. A scale model is great—at least you get a three-dimensional feel for how a project will look, but a full-sized mock-up is best. Use any cheap, easy-to-work material like particleboard, scrapwood or even cardboard. Nail it, screw it or use hot-melt glue—whatever is fast and easy. Just make sure that the dimensions are accurate. This is your last opportunity to make any significant changes.

4. Cutting list: This lists every part in your project with its description, width, thickness and length. Be sure to include any practice pieces you might need to use for setting up jigs, setting bit heights and the like. It's much easier to prepare these along with the actual parts than to try to duplicate them exactly later.

5. Selection: Now decide which piece of wood to use for each part. Start with the most visible parts, and use the nicest-looking wood where it will count. Work your way down to the parts that show little or not at all. Spending a little extra time now will have a great effect on how the finished piece looks. Don't be afraid to waste a little material to get the look you want—it's worth it.

6. Preparation of stock: After rough-cutting all of the parts with a bandsaw or jigsaw, it's time to mill or prepare stock. This consists of flattening one face and edge on the jointer, getting the stock to the desired thickness with a thickness planer and cutting to width and length with a saw.

Preparation of stock is not exciting, but it's important that you do it right. Quality furniture begins with parts that are flat, square and true.

7. Mark out and cut joints: If you're cutting joints by hand, mark out the joinery now. If you're cutting the joinery with a machine, now is the time to set up your jigs and stops, using the practice pieces you have already prepared.

8. Shaping: After cutting the joints, do any shaping required. This could mean rounding over edges, tapering legs, hogging out a seat or almost anything else. Whenever possible, cut all your joinery before you alter the shape of the part. Jigs and fences are much easier to set up for straight and square stock than they are for tapered or curved parts.

9. Finish inside surfaces: Inside corners can be difficult to finish and not much fun. It's much easier to apply the finish to the parts while they're still separate than after they're assembled. Also, glue squeeze-out on raw wood can create finishing problems. If the surfaces are prefinished, simply let the squeeze-out dry, and pop it off with a sharp chisel. Glue will not stick to the finish.

10. Subassembly: Chances are you'll have a subassembly or two to take care of before final assembly. Each one will usually create more inside surfaces that should be finished before moving on.

11. Final assembly and finishing: By now, there should be very little finishing to do. Glue and clamp the piece together, finish the outside and stand back to admire a job well-done.

THREE

Engineering Furniture to Last

For a piece of furniture to last, it has to meet two basic criteria. First, it has to be built to withstand years of use and abuse—otherwise it will fall apart. Second, it has to look good—otherwise it will eventually get thrown out. When one criterion is met but not the other, the piece is perhaps saved for a while longer, but not forever. A beautifully proportioned old chair with all its joints pulling apart might get consigned to a corner, or even fixed; but badly designed joints can only be fixed so many times before they're unsalvageable. On the other hand, a really ugly sideboard that's "still perfectly useable" might stick around for many years—that is until a move or a big church sale. Meeting both these criteria when building a piece is a complex matter. You'll find solutions throughout the book, but the material in this chapter addresses the issues head-on.

Paul Harrell addresses the subtleties of grain orientation to make a harmonious piece of furniture. Reading the grain, so to speak, and thinking about what it will say on the finished piece isn't as ethereal as it might seem. Harrell gives strong visual evidence that there are right ways and odd ways to orient grain in a piece. The odd, random ways will always produce a piece that annoys the eye.

On the other side of the equation, John Wagner clears the smoke and mirrors around the question of the relative strength of several common joints. He reports on tests run by two other woodworkers to determine which joints held up best compressed by a hydraulic ram. The results are slightly surprising—a three-biscuit joint does better in some respects than a mortise-and-tenon joint.

Perhaps the most difficult type of furniture to build to last is outdoor furniture. It has to withstand the elements, from searing heat and humidity in the summer to cold, and perhaps snow and ice, in the winter. This is a tall order for any material, but Jim Tolpin offers some tips that make it very possible to build wood outdoor furniture that last. The keys are to choose a finish wisely, one that offers the maximum protection, and to design joints so that they shed rather than trap moisture.

DESIGNING ALONG THE GRAIN

by Paul Harrell

Grain control. The wood for this desk was cut so that the grain follows and accentuates its concave front, convex sides and flared legs.

If someone remarks on the grain in a piece of furniture, they are usually responding to something exotic: wood with wild quilted figure or vibrant bands of color, perhaps a piece of quartersawn oak with a sunrise of medullary rays streaming across it. Most furniture does without such arresting patterns, but the visual power of the grain is still at work. Even in furniture made with the plainest wood, the grain pattern can

have a profound impact on the success of the design.

On the drawing board, a design is all outlines. When you build the piece in wood, in effect you draw a lot more lines on it. Selecting and orienting the wood to control those new lines is a key part of the design process. Often, the difference between enhancing and undermining a design is just a matter of rotating a leg blank 90° before you saw it, or spending a minute or two laying out a group of stretchers before cutting them out. Selecting and sawing wood with care is like good joinery: Neither will rescue a bad design, but they are both necessary to turn a good idea into fine furniture.

Same dimensions, different design

I made the two tables shown here to demonstrate how deeply a few small changes in the selection and sawing of wood can affect a design. The tables have the same materials, the same details and the same dimensions. But they are not the same design.

In the table on the facing page, the three drawer fronts are cut from the same piece of wood, and as the face grain flows across them, it curves upward in the middle, accentuating the concave shape. The stretcher below the drawers is sawn so that its face grain also picks up this inward bow. The grain of the convex side apron is continuous with the front, having been cut from the same board. But it was sawn so that its face grain curves downward, to emphasize the apron's outward bow. And in the legs, the grain sweeps out at the bottom to follow their flare.

But in the table at right, two of the drawers match fairly well while the third is from a different plank. The face grain on the side apron goes any which way. And as the legs curve outward, the grain sweeps inward.

If I've succeeded, nothing in the first table calls attention to itself; all the shapes seem clear; it has what English furniture maker Edward Barnsley called repose. In the second table, the haphazard choice of wood makes the piece seem at odds with itself.

On the following pages, I've presented a few techniques for predicting and controlling grain. I don't think there is always one right way to have the grain flow across a piece of furniture. The point is not to let it be an accident.

Grain completes the picture _____

A good shape on the drawing board can be emphasized or undermined by the wood grain. A careful craftsman can learn to predict and control the grain.

Grain dead. Mismatched drawer fronts and aprons, and legs with grain that fights the curve rob this desk of its repose.

Arranging the grain for wooden legs

Because legs are seen from all sides, it is important that the grain on adjacent faces be compatible. For a straight or tapered leg, you can get the same grain pattern on all four faces by cutting the leg blank so that the grain (as viewed on the end) runs diagonally from one corner to the other. Cutting the leg with the end grain parallel instead of diagonal results in two faces with straight grain and two with curving grain.

If the legs will be curved, the diagonal pattern of the end grain should run toward the outside corners of the legs. This allows the grain lines to follow the shape of the legs instead of running counter to it. If the legs are oriented incorrectly, the grain lines will be cut as the curve is sawn. The grain will appear to fight the curve of the leg, and in addition, the grain will be shorter, and the legs weaker.

Orienting the grain for leg blanks

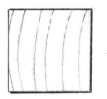

Parallel end grain results in a leg with two straight-grained faces and two wavy-grained faces.

Diagonal end grain results in a leg with straight grain on all four faces.

Orienting the grain to follow a curved leg

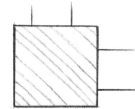

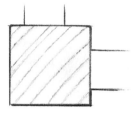

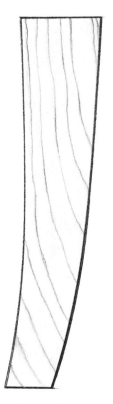

With end grain diagonal but running side to side, the face grain fights the curve of the leg.

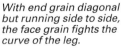

With diagonal end grain running outward, the face grain will follow the curve of the leg.

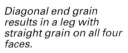

When I want to cut blanks for legs, I try to find planks that have diagonal grain at one or both edges. It's possible to get legs with the right grain from a thick quartersawn plank, but you have to make a lot of sawdust to do it, and you lose a board better suited as a tabletop, cabinet case or veneer.

Finding legs in lumber

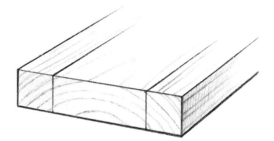

You can often find leg stock at the edges of flat-sawn planks.

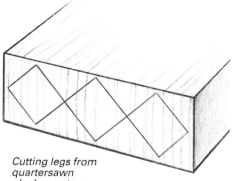

Cutting legs from quartersawn planks wastes wood.

Grain design for doors

When I'm building frame-and-panel doors, I want wood for the stiles and rails that will frame the panel, not compete with it. I try to keep the pieces as uniform as possible, never mixing flat and quartersawn pieces.

Just as with curved aprons and stretchers (see following page), doors that curve inward or outward across their faces will benefit from having rails whose grain accentuates the curve.

After cutting out pieces for a door or doors, I always experiment with different arrangements of the parts. The same pieces turned a different way will often have very different appearances.

Framing grain

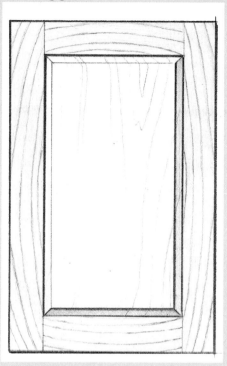

Turned outward, curved grain fights a frame's shape.

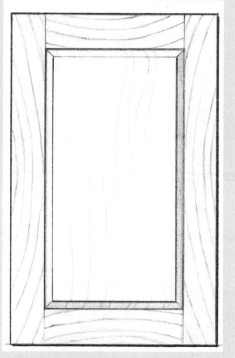

Curved grain creating a circular pattern gives a frame unity.

Sawing wood for aprons and stretchers

I look for mild, fairly straight-grained stock for straight aprons and stretchers. The various pieces don't have to be identical, but I avoid mixing widely different grain patterns. If the wood has a strong pattern of bands or streaks of color running through it, it's worth the effort to match the aprons end-to-end so that the pattern is continuous.

For curved aprons and stretchers, it's important that the face grain accentuate the shape. On a concave apron, face grain that curves upward in the middle like a frown will reinforce the curve of the piece; face grain that runs perfectly horizontal will reduce the apparent curve; face grain that curves downward in the middle like a smile will fight the curve.

When sawing a curved part, pick a blank with diagonal end grain. If you cut it with the end grain running up from front to back, the face grain will accentuate the sweep of the curve, whether convex or concave. If the end grain slopes the wrong way, the face grain will work against the curve.

The amount of curve in the face grain can be predicted by the amount of slope in the end grain. A steep upward slope in the end grain will yield an exaggerated curve in the face grain.

Grain that flows from piece to piece

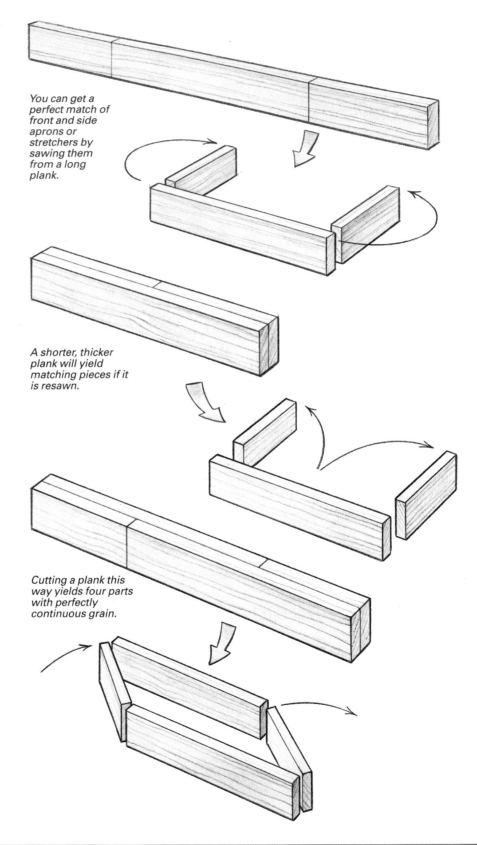

You can get a perfect match of front and side aprons or stretchers by sawing them from a long plank.

A shorter, thicker plank will yield matching pieces if it is resawn.

Cutting a plank this way yields four parts with perfectly continuous grain.

Accentuating a bow

When cutting a concave or convex piece, choose a blank with diagonal end grain and orient it so that the end grain slopes up from front to back. The face grain will accentuate the curve of the cut.

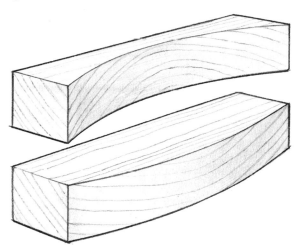

Undermining a bow

The same part oriented with the end grain sloping the other way produces face grain that runs counter to the curve.

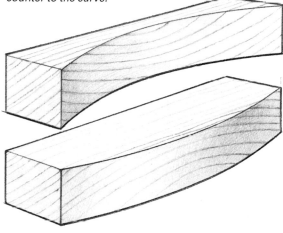

Stronger curves

Steeply sloped end grain produces an exaggerated curve in the face grain.

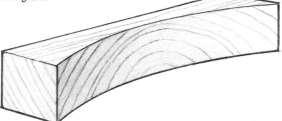

Dealing with drawers

I often resaw thick veneers for drawer fronts from a single plank, but even these will vary subtly in grain and color. The thick veneers sawn from the top of the plank have tighter face grain than the ones toward the bottom, which have a wide flat-sawn section in the center. If the color is consistent, putting the fronts with the tighter grain at the bottom of the bureau should give the piece a solid, grounded feeling. If the flat-sawn center section is darker, as it will be in some woods, these fronts might look better at the bottom.

Resawing for drawers

Resawing veneer from a single plank for drawer fronts ensures a good color match.

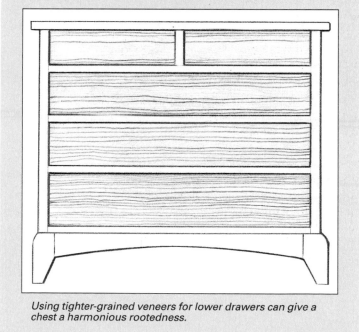

Using tighter-grained veneers for lower drawers can give a chest a harmonious rootedness.

FINISHES FOR OUTDOOR FURNITURE

by Jim Tolpin

Choose wood carefully for unfinished exterior furniture. Plantation teak, used in this bench, is a good choice because it's naturally rot-resistant and turns a beautiful silver gray. Some other durable woods are white oak, cypress and cedar. These woods are easily maintained by occasionally scrubbing away dirt and mildew. Bronze caps protect the bench's feet from standing water.

With the time and effort required to construct a piece of outdoor furniture, an obvious question is what finish will protect it from the sun, rain and cold. The answers range from doing nothing to spraying on a coat of catalyzed linear polyurethane, the same stuff used to paint 747 jumbo jets. The choice of whether to finish or not to finish is not just a question of protecting the wood. You must decide how you want your outdoor furniture to look over its lifespan and how much time you're willing to invest to maintain this appearance year after year.

No finish: carefully choose the wood

Deciding not to finish means choosing a wood that is stable and rot resistant. It also means being willing to accept a coarse-textured piece of furniture that can vary in color from silver gray to dark gray or brown. The advantage of not finishing is the minimal maintenance required to keep the surface clean.

Some good woods for outdoor use are redwood, cypress and cedars. I especially like Port Orford cedar for its workability and light color. These species contain natural pesticides in their chemical makeup, and all are incredibly resistant to rot. However, these relatively soft woods offer little impact resistance, and they have been extensively over-harvested. But in recent years, several companies have formed to recycle old timbers.

For a harder wood that will stand up to bumps, choose white oak or black locust. These woods build up tyloses, a bubble-like formation that blocks the penetration of water into the cell structure, making them particularly well-suited for outdoor use. Two other woods usually associated with indoor furniture, black cherry and walnut, surprisingly rate with the cedars in decay resistance because of their closed-cell structure. Also, Pacific yew is a beautiful wood that outperforms even redwood in rot resistance. But these species move quite a bit with changes in moisture content, making them prone to surface checking and warping if left unfinished.

For outstanding beauty with exceptional stability and rot resistance, nothing can beat Honduras mahogany or teak. These woods age to a gorgeous silver gray after only six months of exposure. But quotas and over-harvesting have driven prices up and availability down. The good news is that plantation teak and other lesser-known species are now being harvested, often from sustainable-yield forestry operations in tropical countries.

Inherent rot resistance is not the only criterion to consider when choosing wood to be used outside. The wood should be air-dried to a maximum 20% moisture content to provide stability and enduring, tight-fitting joints. In addition, select the stock from the heart of the tree, avoiding the sapwood. The sapwood contains—you guessed it—sap. And sap is full of sugar, a wood bug's breakfast of champions.

Selecting the right finish

To get a color other than gray and to minimize the inevitable surface checking of exposed wood, you can coat the wood with penetrating oils, varnishes, paints or epoxies. Clear penetrating oils and water sealers designed for exterior use contain ultraviolet (UV) filters and bring out the natural color of the wood. The UV filters help shield the wood from solar radiation, which destroys the lignin in the wood and reduces the wood's ability to hang on to the finish. Transparent stains and washes enhance the natural color or impart their own tint.

Finally, you can seal the wood entirely under a pigmented gloss topcoat—I call this paint around my shop. Paint is the right finish if you want to shield the wood from sunlight completely.

To test the longevity of the commonly available oils, stains and water seals, outdoor furnituremaker Mark Singer of Santa Barbara, Calif., subjected dozens of coated wood samples to grueling tests in an accelerated environmental chamber. After the equivalent of one year in a harsh environ-

Paint can't overcome poor design. This unlined, wood planter box is destined to fail because the moist soil holds water against the wood, allowing it to seep into the joints, and these joints aren't designed to drain water. The unprotected end grain of the feet also wicks up water from the puddles in which the planter stands.

Joinery to cope with water

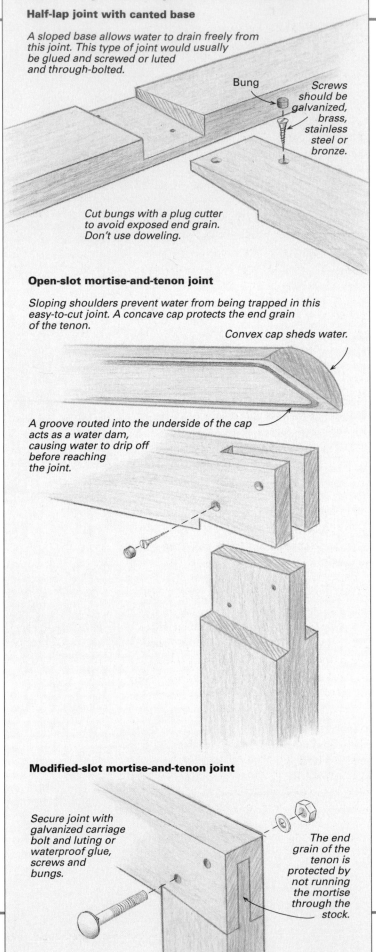

Half-lap joint with canted base

A sloped base allows water to drain freely from this joint. This type of joint would usually be glued and screwed or luted and through-bolted.

Bung

Screws should be galvanized, brass, stainless steel or bronze.

Cut bungs with a plug cutter to avoid exposed end grain. Don't use doweling.

Open-slot mortise-and-tenon joint

Sloping shoulders prevent water from being trapped in this easy-to-cut joint. A concave cap protects the end grain of the tenon.

Convex cap sheds water.

A groove routed into the underside of the cap acts as a water dam, causing water to drip off before reaching the joint.

Modified-slot mortise-and-tenon joint

Secure joint with galvanized carriage bolt and luting or waterproof glue, screws and bungs.

The end grain of the tenon is protected by not running the mortise through the stock.

Building to last

The type and quality of the finish and the material from which outdoor furniture is made contribute immensely to its beauty and to its durability. But the best of coatings and materials can be destroyed by construction techniques that trap water within the furniture. Trapped water nourishes voracious parasites that can reduce wood to a sponge cake of half-digested cellulose.

With this happy thought in mind, I'm inspired to find ways to build outdoor furniture with a second line of defense. I've learned that a structure exposed to the elements needs to be built with waterproof glues, joints that shed water without sacrificing strength and with fasteners that won't rust away.

Fasteners and adhesives

When you must attach components to one another, use a fastener made from (or coated with) a non-ferrous metal. Not only does iron rust, eventually crumbling to dust, but also it causes corrosive damage to the wood, especially to acidic woods like oak. If I don't care about appearance, I'll use a hot-dipped galvanized fastener. If appearance is important, I'll choose either stainless steel or bronze. In some applications, such as attaching thin slats to a framework, I'll use the boatbuilding technique of riveting with copper tacks and roves, a dished washer over which the end of the tack is peened.

Woodworkers can choose from three types of outdoor adhesives: a water-mixed plastic-resin glue, a two-part epoxy resin and Titebond II, a new one-part adhesive that the manufacturer claims will stand up to most outdoor applications except submersion. Although I've yet to try it, the convenience of an adhesive that you don't have to mix is mighty appealing. I've used Weldwood's plastic-resin glue for years. Unlike epoxy, the plastic-resin glue is not strong across gaps. But I'm allergic to epoxy, and I don't like its sensitivity to temperature during setup. For oily woods such as teak, however, epoxy remains the best choice.

Water-shedding construction

Whenever possible, I design joints so water can drain out. The canted base of the half-lap joint, as shown in the drawing at right, prevents water from accumulating under the overlapping tongue. A slot mortise-and-tenon joint, as shown in the drawing, is easy to cut, and its angled shoulders drain water from the joint. This joint exposes the tenon's end grain on a horizontal surface and should be capped, or the tenon should be stopped short, as shown in the drawing. Note that the cap has a convex top surface to shed water and a groove along its bottom edge. The groove acts as a water dam, encouraging the water to drip at this point, rather than continuing to the joint area.

Other defenses

As added insurance against water finding a home between two non-glued wood surfaces, I coat the joint's mating surfaces with a luting compound before fastening them together. Traditionally, pine tar was used for this purpose, though modern adhesive caulking compounds and specialized marine bedding compounds, such as Dolfinite by Woolsey/Z-Spar, have largely replaced pine tar.

My last defense is common sense. Leaving unprotected legs of outdoor furniture sitting in moist soil is asking for trouble. I seal the end grain of legs with paint and set them on bricks or gravel for good drainage. I also avoid leaving my furniture sitting unprotected under blistering summer sun or under a winter's worth of snow. A tarp can protect your furniture year round when not in use, but in the winter, it's best to bring it indoors. This is why I've designed many of my chairs and tables to fold for storage. Finally, if I do decide to put a finish on the structure, I am then committed to keeping that finish intact.

ment, not a single sample was free from significant deterioration. Singer's suspicions were confirmed. Unless these types of finishes are constantly renewed, they loose both their protective functions and their decorative effects, and the surface of the wood eventually turns blotchy.

Gloss topcoats deliver the maximum durability in a clear finish, especially in harsh sun-drenched environments. The additives that turn a gloss finish to semigloss or satin soften the finish coat, reduce UV reflection and decrease longevity. Traditional spar varnish has no peer in bringing out the beauty of wood. It's durable, long lasting in a harsh marine environment and is easily renewable. As long as a varnished surface is regularly maintained (at least once a year), the color of the wood will last indefinitely. Regular maintenance includes touching up nicks and worn spots, and sanding and reapplying two new topcoats before signs of graying show up.

Modern urethane varnishes can last at least twice as long as spar varnishes, though their intrinsic hardness makes them significantly more difficult to repair. The new water-based urethane exterior varnishes are as hard and durable as their petroleum-based brethren. In addition, water-based products are less toxic during application, they recoat within hours and they are non-yellowing. None of the urethanes, however, can equal the distinctive rich glow of spar varnish.

The ultimate in long-lasting protection and gloss retention are the aerospace industry's catalyzed, two-part, linear polyurethane finishes. This amazing stuff, when properly applied over an epoxy undercoating, dries 50% harder than spar varnish and reportedly lasts up to five years in marine conditions. But the price is high. To coat 100 sq. ft. costs about $150.

Paint is, by far, the most protective and longest-lasting coating you can put on a piece of wood destined to live outside. The higher the gloss and the lighter the color, the better the protection. The gloss reflects the sun's harmful rays, and the light colors absorb less of the heat that can break down the paint film.

Applying exterior finishes

Pros use certain tricks to get outstanding results every time. While these tricks may not make you a pro overnight, they are sure to improve your results. But first, you might as well get used to hearing this timeless platitude: A finish is only as good as its preparation. This is as true for simple wipe-on stains as for the most expensive catalyzed urethane paint.

Preparing the surface

Preparation means well-sanded surfaces, including sanding after raising the grain with a damp rag. Hardwoods need only be sanded to 120-grit, as long as all sanding scratches from the previous grit have been removed. Softwoods should be sanded to 220-grit. Never use steel wool to smooth wood destined for the outdoors. The remnants of steel in the pores of the wood will rust and ruin the finish.

Preparation also means well-cleaned surfaces. Wash off oily handprints with a rag dampened with thinner and follow with a light sanding. Before applying the first coat of a primer or a sealer, thoroughly vacuum the wood, and then use a tack rag to wipe away any remaining particles.

Most finishes can be put on directly from the can by brushing, wiping or spraying. The only trick is to not recoat too quickly. Follow the manufacturer's directions. Some finishes, especially the penetrating oils, should never be applied in direct sunlight. Bill Kennedy of Specialty Furniture Co., a manufacturer of outdoor furniture in Mt. Pleasant, Mich., says that sun-heated wood can bleed out the finish, which then glazes on the surface. Because oil finishes are not designed to stand on the surface like a varnish, they quickly crack and craze, and eventually peel off, requiring stripping and sanding to a clean, solid surface before refinishing.

Applying varnish

For a clear, smooth and uniform coating of varnish, follow these basic practices:

• Mix varnish by gently stirring with a paddle, never by shaking it. The resultant bubbles end up as holes and bumps in the surface film.

• Never use the finish straight from the can. Instead, strain it through a paper cone filter into a clean bucket.

• Use professional varnish brushes made from fine China bristle or badger hair grouped into an oval cross section. These brushes cost a small fortune, but they contribute immensely to the illusion that your varnish job had a pro behind the brush. Never use your varnish brushes for paint.

• Avoid varnishing in cool, damp conditions or in direct sunlight. Cold prevents the film from hardening properly, and the sun's heat hardens the outer surface of the film too quickly, resulting in wrinkles and sags. Also, gases in the warmed wood bubble up through the finish, leaving pock marks.

I'm pretty good at applying varnish, but Julia Maynard, a full-time, freelance painter and varnisher in Port Townsend, Wash., is the best I've seen. Here are her recommendations for a durable professional-looking varnish finish:

• Use a marine-grade spar varnish with ultraviolet (UV) filters. Beginners would do well with a less dense, less expensive variety such as Interlux's Schooner Varnish (see the sources of supply box). It flows easily and sets up quickly to reduce wrinkling and sagging problems, and it holds up nearly as well as the most expensive varieties.

• To extend the life of the varnish coating, especially when applied to oily woods such as teak, use a volatile and highly penetrative undercoat. The best is Flashbond 300, made by X-I-M Products.

• To build up enough UV filtration to really protect the wood, especially in sunny climates, apply at least five coats of varnish. Apply each coat carefully—think of each layer as the final coat. To avoid lap marks, apply the varnish from the dry area back to the wet area.

• Use a hand block, never a power sander, to sand to 280-grit between coats, removing all brush marks and other imperfections.

• Never use thinner to clean off the dust between coats (it reduces adhesion). Instead, vacuum and wipe with a tack rag.

• For a super final finish, go to a sixth coat. But first, sand the gloss off the last coat with 320-grit wet-or-dry paper, being careful not to cut through the topcoat. Clean away the dust, and apply the last coat with all the skill you've acquired over the first five coatings.

Applying paint

As with varnish, there are similar precautions to take for a durable, first-class paint job. Don't shake—stir the paint. Don't use it straight from the can; filter it into a clean bucket. Apply paint at room temperature and out of the direct sun. And finally, use a good China bristle brush to apply paint.

Follow these steps to achieve a top-notch paint finish:

• Fill countersunk screw holes with wood plugs (bungs), fixing them in place with shellac or varnish. Don't glue the bungs if you might want to get to the screws again.

• Sand the surfaces to 120-grit for hardwoods, or 220-grit for softwoods. Raise the grain with a damp rag at the 100-grit stage, and then sand off the protruding fibers.

• Fill small defects with a glazing compound (be sure it is compatible with your paint) or a specialized surfacing compound such as Interlux's #257.

• Vacuum and tack the surfaces thoroughly. Julia Maynard then wipes the surfaces with a rag dampened with isopropyl alcohol to pick up fine dust and draw any surface moisture out of the wood.

• Apply the primer coats. Yes, that's plural. Build up the paint thickness with three coats of primer. Maynard, and many other professional exterior painters, do not, however, recommend using standard primers. They think the surface left by primers is too chalky for the best topcoat adhesion. They prefer a thinned-down semi-gloss topcoat paint. White is okay for most colors, but gray is best for low-hide colors like red and yellow. Sand between primer coats with 150-grit paper to remove all brush streaks, runs and drips.

• Sand the last coat of primer to 400-grit, clean up, and apply the gloss topcoat, always brushing from the dry area back to the wet area to avoid lap marks.

To make all this worthwhile, buy the most expensive enamel. It will only be a few bucks more per gallon. Oil or latex-based enamels are about equal in durability. But don't bust the bank on marine oil-based enamels unless you know the furniture will be exposed to salt air, intense sunshine and an occasional splash of gasoline.

No finish lasts forever. This white oak door, built for a client seven years ago by the author and finished with six coats of spar varnish, shows the effects of exposure and neglect. The finish at the top of the door, protected by the overhanging wall, is still in good shape, but at the fully exposed bottom, the finish is completely gone.

CHOOSING THE STRONGEST JOINERY FOR DOORS

by John D. Wagner

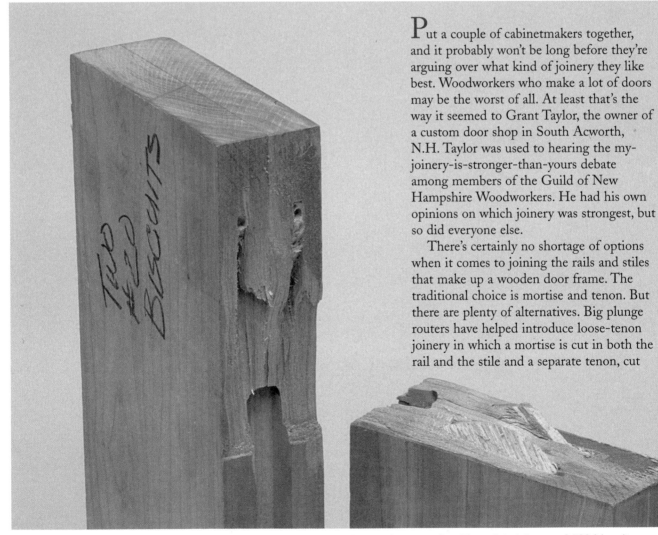

Put a couple of cabinetmakers together, and it probably won't be long before they're arguing over what kind of joinery they like best. Woodworkers who make a lot of doors may be the worst of all. At least that's the way it seemed to Grant Taylor, the owner of a custom door shop in South Acworth, N.H. Taylor was used to hearing the my-joinery-is-stronger-than-yours debate among members of the Guild of New Hampshire Woodworkers. He had his own opinions on which joinery was strongest, but so did everyone else.

There's certainly no shortage of options when it comes to joining the rails and stiles that make up a wooden door frame. The traditional choice is mortise and tenon. But there are plenty of alternatives. Big plunge routers have helped introduce loose-tenon joinery in which a mortise is cut in both the rail and the stile and a separate tenon, cut

Biscuits make a strong joint. Among the strongest joints tested were those made with a plate joiner and #20 biscuits. How the joint would fare after repeated freeze-thaw cycles is another matter.

from stock run off on the tablesaw, joins the two. Dowel construction is much faster than mortise and tenon but is generally considered weaker. Biscuit joiners, which cut football-shaped slots in rail and stile for pressed-wood splines, may be the fastest method of all. Each method had something to offer. Some were faster and less labor-intensive; others appealed to traditionalists. But reliable information on just how strong these joints actually were and how well they'd stand up over time, seemed to be in short supply.

Eventually, Taylor had heard enough. He decided to find out which joint really does make the strongest door. He got in touch with Ben Brungraber, the resident engineer at Benson Woodworking in Alstead, N.H., for help. Brungraber had been interested in the question ever since writing his doctoral dissertation on timber joint strength, and together, the two devised a testing procedure they hoped would settle the argument for good.

The result? Biscuited joints were the strongest, but mortise-and-tenon construction still may be the best choice. To know why, you'll have to know more about how the tests were run.

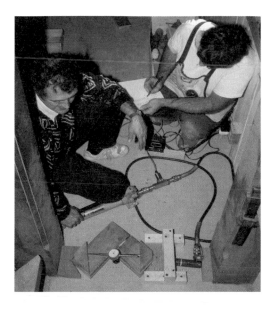

Taking door joints to the breaking point—Ben Brungraber, left, applies hydraulic pressure to a mocked-up door frame joint.

Building the joints and a test bed

It would be a stretch to call these tests a rigorous scientific examination. Sure, the samples were well-made and the tests run carefully. But a truly definitive study was far beyond the facilities and time that Taylor and Brungraber had to work with. Even with its limits, though, their work may help settle an argument or two.

Taylor and Brungraber had a pretty simple idea: Make up a number of different

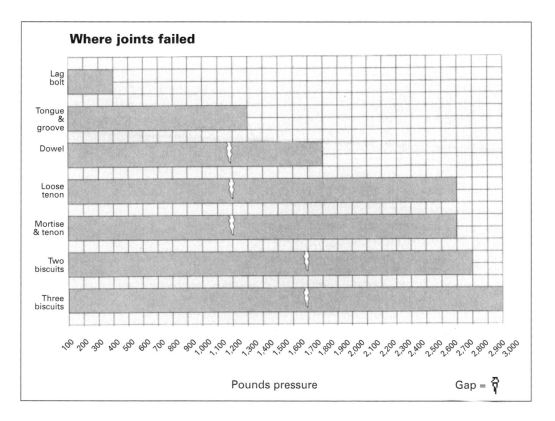

Where joints failed

Lag bolt
Tongue & groove
Dowel
Loose tenon
Mortise & tenon
Two biscuits
Three biscuits

100 200 300 400 500 600 700 800 900 1,000 1,100 1,200 1,300 1,400 1,500 1,600 1,700 1,800 1,900 2,000 2,100 2,200 2,300 2,400 2,500 2,600 2,700 2,800 2,900 3,000

Pounds pressure   Gap =

Loose tenon proves to be good joinery—It took 2,700 lbs. of pressure to force the loose-tenon joint to fail, making it one of the top performers in the test.

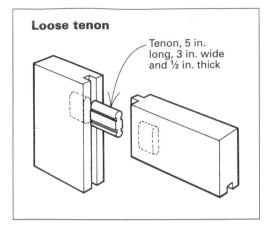

Loose tenon

Tenon, 5 in. long, 3 in. wide and ½ in. thick

kinds of joints; then bend them until they broke. The instrument of torture was a 1-in. hydraulic ram hooked up to a device showing how much pressure was being applied. Brungraber had used the same device to break apart massive timber joints in strength tests. The pair devised a floor-mounted jig that would hold the mocked-up door frame joints between two hefty timber posts (see the photo p. 53).

Setting up the joint tests

Taylor built seven different types of joints, each one imitating where the rail and stile of a door frame meets above a hinge. Each joint consisted of a stile section 12 in. long and a rail section 7½ in. long. Taylor routed ½-in.-wide by ⅝-in.-deep grooves in the inside edges of both rail-and-stile sections where a panel would normally go.

A tongue was cut in each rail section to mate with the groove in the stile, as shown in the drawings here. Each of these basic joints was then modified with the addition of other joinery, such as dowels, a loose tenon, lag bolts or a traditional mortise and tenon. All the wood used was clear cherry (two pieces of cherry were face-glued together to make the 1⁷⁄₁₆ in. thickness of rail-and-stile sections). All the joints were glued up with Elmer's yellow glue and then allowed to dry for two weeks.

Taylor also made calculations to ensure that the glued surface area of the dowels used in one joint was the same surface area as the loose tenon or mortise and tenon used in another. His intent was to make the test as even as he could. In all, the joints includ-

ed a mortise and tenon, a loose tenon, a dowel joint, a joint lag bolted together with no glue, a ½-in. by ⅝-in. tongue and groove and two biscuited joints, one with two #20 biscuits, the other with three #20 biscuits.

Doors sag toward the lock side, so Taylor decided to test each joint in compression. Once mounted in the testing jig, the joint would be compressed by Brungraber's hydraulic ram to simulate the strain that a sagging door would impose on the joint.

Taylor used a dial indicator sensitive to 0.001-in. movement to track the joint's deflection under pressure. As Brungraber applied pressure in 100-lb. increments with a hydraulic pump, Taylor recorded the correlation between the joint's movement and the pressure.

Tests measured three things: the joint's overall resistance to deflection, how much pressure it took to open up a gap in the joint and when the joint failed. By plotting the deflection and hydraulic pressure information on a graph, Taylor and Brungraber could track each joint's performance against the others (see the chart on p. 53).

Testing the joints

With curious woodworkers hovering nearby, Taylor and Brungraber loaded the first joint into the jig and brought the hydraulic jack to tension. Because no one was sure how the joint would react or how it would fail, nerves ran a bit high until the first test showed that most failures were incremental, not violent (there were three exceptions,

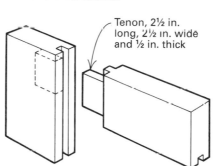

Mortise and tenon

Tenon, 2½ in. long, 2½ in. wide and ½ in. thick

High strength in a traditional joint— The mortise-and-tenon connection showed good overall strength and isn't likely to fail completely or suddenly, making the joint the first choice of timber framers.

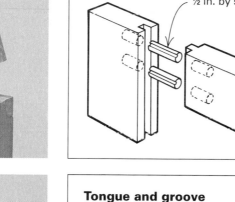

Dowels

½ in. by 5⁹⁄₁₆ in.

Dowels may not be the best choice— The doweled joint may have relied on the tongue-and-groove connection for much of its strength. Once the stile split, the dowels pulled out without much resistance.

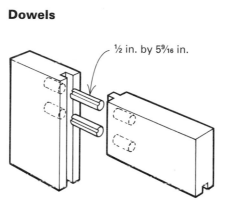

Tongue and groove

½ in. by ⅝ in.

Tongue-and-groove joint shows surprising strength—Even without extra reinforcement, the simple tongue-and-groove joint took 1,300 lbs. of pressure before it shattered into two pieces.

which I'll tell you about later). Here's a summary of what they discovered.

Loose tenon

The loose tenon measured 5 in. long, 3 in. wide and ¹⁄₂ in. thick, with two glue grooves cut on each side. The joint deflected just over ⁷⁄₁₆ in. before it showed a slight gap at 1,200 lbs. pressure. The joint failed outright at 2,700 lbs. But upon examining the failure, Taylor and Brungraber found that the tenon

didn't fail. Instead, the stile itself split, allowing the loose tenon (not starved of glue, it turned out) to be pulled out slowly (see the photo on the facing page).

Mortise and tenon

The traditional, square-cornered mortise-and-tenon joint showed above-average resistance to deflection and good resistance to gapping. Like the loose tenon, the joint didn't gap until 1,200 lbs. of pressure had

been applied. It failed outright at 2,700 lbs. (see the top photo on p. 57). But it deflected $7/16$ in. more than the loose tenon at the same point of failure.

Dowel

The two $1/2$-in. dowels each measured $5^9/16$ in. long. The joint failed at 1,800 lbs. of pressure, with a gap forming at about 1,200 lbs. (see the center photo on p. 57). Taylor had grooved the dowels to promote glue distribution. Even so, the dowels appeared a bit glue-starved and probably would have performed better had the glue been spread over mating surfaces more evenly.

Taylor and Brungraber were interested to see that the $5/8$-in. tongue and groove in this joint never failed. The joint broke when the stile split along the grain. Once the grain began ripping apart, the dowels simply pulled out without much resistance.

Tongue and groove

Just for the heck of it, Taylor and Brungraber decided to test the $5/8$-in. tongue-and-groove joint by itself. It was a lot stronger than people thought it would be. There was no gapping until the joint shattered outright at 1,300 lbs. of pressure (see the bottom photo on p. 57). Here, too, the joint itself didn't fail; it forced a failure along the stile's grain and broke the wood.

Lag bolts

The two $1/4$-in. lags extended $1^3/4$ in. into the stile. This joint was the worst performer by far (see the photo above). A gap opened in the joint at 400 lbs. with each stroke of the jack producing more and more deflection. It was a dramatic illustration of how little holding power threads have in end grain.

Biscuits

The two biscuited joints were a little different from the others in that they didn't have the $5/8$-in. tongue and groove—just a butt joint. The first biscuit joint had two #20 biscuits, each one inserted $1/2$ in. from each face of the frame. The second joint included

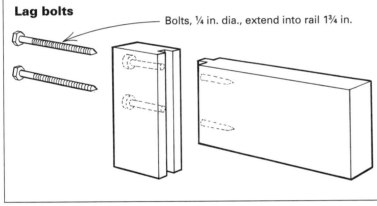

Lag bolts

Bolts, ¼ in. dia., extend into rail 1¾ in.

Lag bolts and no glue make for the weakest joint—The lag-bolt joint clearly demonstrated the failure of screw threads to hold in end grain. The bolts began losing their grip when the joint gapped at a mere 400 lbs. of pressure.

a third biscuit, inserted between the original two. Both joints behaved almost identically. Both gapped at 1,700 lbs. (the two-biscuit joint deflected 0.032 in. before it gapped, and the three-biscuit joint deflected 0.029 in. before it gapped). The two-biscuit joint failed with a dramatic explosion at 2,800 lbs. pressure (see the photo on p. 52), and the three-biscuit joint failed at 3,000 lbs. pressure with nearly identical deflection (see the photo at right).

In the three-biscuit joint, the biscuits didn't fail. Rather, they forced a failure along the grain of the stile. In other words, the joint was stronger than the wood itself. In the two-biscuit joint, one of the biscuits split, causing a shear failure in the second biscuit. After that, the glued butt joint quickly separated where it was in tension at the top of the joint.

Taylor and Brungraber think that the biscuits themselves in the two-biscuit joint failed around 1,700 lbs., with the glued butt joint giving the holding power until outright failure at 2,800 to 3,000 lbs. Brungraber said the biscuit joints showed wonderful overall strength and resistance to deflection. But in wet-dry or freeze-thaw cycles, the part of the joint without biscuits would eventually fail, and the joint's strength would be compromised as it became solely dependent on the biscuits themselves.

Overall appraisal

So what should you use in your doors? Doors won't take the kind of abuse these tests delivered, but the choice for Brungraber and Taylor is a loose-tenon or traditional mortise-and-tenon joint.

Though the failure of the biscuit joints occurred at nearly the same overall pressure, the biscuit joints failed completely, snapping suddenly into two pieces. Comparatively, the loose tenon and the mortise and tenon first gapped, and then they failed, but the joint stayed physically intact, with the rail and stile still attached to each other. Brungraber says that this is why mortise-and-tenon joints are the joints used in timber framing. Even while the joints fail, they fight every step of the way. The failure in a mortise-

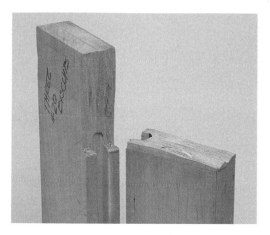

Third biscuit adds little strength— Adding a third biscuit to the joint made no significant improvement in the joint's performance. Close examination reveals the wood failed before the biscuits.

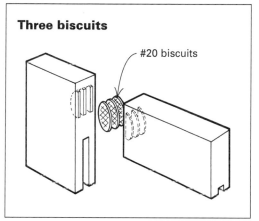

Three biscuits

#20 biscuits

and-tenon joint is rarely as complete and sudden as what they saw in the biscuit-joint failures or the failure of the 5/8-in. tongue-and-groove joint.

The overall best joint, the one that Taylor suspected was the strongest and the one he uses in his custom doors, is the loose tenon. The joint began to open up at the same point as the dowel joint and the mortise and tenon, but the loose-tenon connection showed continued resistance to deflection and good overall strength.

The other graphic lesson found in these joint failures was the essential importance straight-grained wood played in all the joints' strength. Most of the joints proved to be stronger than the wood itself (this is shown by how many of the joints were tenacious enough to force a failure along the stile or rail's grain). Using straight-grained wood will invariably strengthen any joint's overall performance, as does careful, thorough gluing.

FOUR

Construction Options for Tables

The previous chapters have by and large dwelt in the land of theory, addressing the issues at hand and offering examples to illustrate a point. This chapter begins a new section of the book, breaking away from the drawing table and diving down into the sawdust to examine the specifics of good construction designs. Here's where you'll find answers to those everyday questions about the best way to do something. You won't find step-by-step instructions (that's in *Woodworking Techniques*), just the solutions.

How long should a dining room table that seats 12 be? Christian Becksvoort answers that and many other such questions about dining-table proportions. He offers specific measurement ranges to make a table comfortable and useful. You'll never have to guess at how much legroom or elbow room each person needs at a table.

Will Neptune approaches the design of tables with drawers from another perspective: that they all can be built in very similar ways, regardless of the style. He tells his students that "there's a Shaker nightstand hidden in every table with drawers." This approach to overall design greatly reduces the complexity of any one piece because the builder has a universal vocabulary of components and techniques.

Garrett Hack lists five good design options for connecting tops to bases. Wood movement is often forgotten in furniture design, and the consequences are cracks. Tabletops, often 3 ft. or more across their width, will shrink and expand considerably through seasonal variations in humidity. A solid attachment between base and top will ensure a crack develops somewhere. Hack offers attachment designs that hold well but take wood movement into consideration. In another section, Hack addresses options for attaching breadboard ends to tabletops. Though it is more time intensive than leaving the ends plain, the batten helps keep tops flat; this is especially important when using flatsawn boards for the top, which tend to cup more than quartersawn boards.

Finally, Christian Becksvoort offers six different ways to support drop leaves. Sagging leaves are a chronic problem in badly designed drop-leaf tables. They render the table almost unusable—and especially interesting from the point of view of the person watching his plate slide off the edge.

Each of these sections compares and contrasts several of the best designs for making one part of a table.

DINING TABLE DESIGN IS NOT AS EASY AS PIE

by Chris Becksvoort

Eating together without rubbing elbows

You can allow a width of 24 inches for each person, but it makes for cramped dining. For more comfortable dining, allow 30 inches. You'll also need at least 12 inches in front of each person. That means adding 24 inches to a table's length if a person is going to sit at each end.

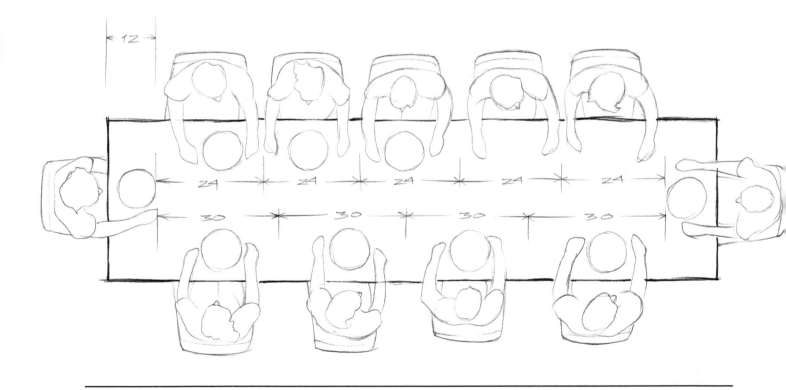

The dining table might just be the most important piece of furniture in our homes. We discuss family matters at it, entertain guests around it, play table games on it, and, of course, we eat at it. It is a homework table, a cook's preparation table, and it is also a family workbench. Yet, its design is often overlooked. Little is written about the form in furniture literature, and the table is frequently taken for granted soon after it is purchased. The dining table gets no respect.

In fact, the only predictably memorable dining table is a bad one. Your guests will remember it if it is too short, too cramped, too small or too big. Put them at a well-designed eating table and the visitors go home happy, but they probably won't remember a thing about the table.

As a designer, I think it is important to accept this rather than fight it. Let your imagination run wild with coffee tables, but keep it firmly in check when it comes to the dinner table. There's no more appropriate place to remember the age-old directive that form should follow function. The primary function of a dining table is to serve as a comfortable place for people to eat. So, a well-designed dining table must follow certain rules, sizes and conventions. When you sit down to design one, you should ask the same questions as you would when you purchase one. How many people will regularly sit at it? What size table will the room accommodate? What shape top do you like? Should it be a pedestal table, a trestle table or a traditional table with four legs and an apron? How can you get a strong table without making it clunky? How high should it be? There's a lot to consider.

Guess who's coming to dinner

The first thing you need to consider is the number of people you want to be able to seat at the table. A 3-foot by 4-foot table might sound like the answer for you. But if you entertain large numbers of people regularly in a huge dining room, the size probably won't be appropriate. On the other hand, if you have a family of four, there is almost no point in having a 14-foot long dining table just to make room for a family reunion every other Thanksgiving.

It's a good idea to consider what else you might want to use your dining room table for. Granted, Aunt Thelma and Uncle Roy might stop by for turkey only every second year, but if you like to sit at the table and spread out the Sunday paper, or build a scale model of "Old Ironsides," a bigger table might be right for you.

Fitting the table to the room

Another important design consideration is the dimensions of the room where the table will sit. Face it, if your dining room or the area where you want to put your table is 8 feet by 10 feet, there's just no way you are going to fit a table to seat 12 people. People sitting at the table have to be able to get in and out of their chairs comfortably, and if they are jammed into a corner of the room or into a wall, they will feel trapped.

In order for the average person to get up from the table—push his chair back and stand up comfortably—he needs about three feet of floor space from the edge of the table to the back of the chair (see the drawing on p. 63). It seems like a lot of space, but it really isn't when you figure that the seats of most chairs, excluding the legs and back, are 16 inches deep. The American Institute of Architects says that 36 inches is the minimum distance to push a chair back. The preferred distance is 44 inches, and for wheelchairs, you should allow at least 54 inches.

One size fits all—most of the time

As a rule of thumb, it is normal to allow 24 inches of tabletop perimeter per person. That does not mean that you could seat 11 people at a 3-foot by 8-foot table, because the ends cannot accommodate one and a half people. Twenty-four inches of table space is the absolute minimum per diner. People just don't like to eat with their elbows pinned to their ribs. Thirty inches is a lot closer to the ideal, and it allows for more gracious dining (see the drawing on the facing page). And if you use any armchairs, 30 inches becomes the minimum.

It's a good idea to figure in an across-the-table depth of 12 inches for each person at the table. Twelve inches is enough for most place mats, silverware, and a dinner plate. Place-setting depth is especially important when designing a rectangular table where people will sit at each end of the table as well as along the sides. When I design a rectangular table, after I've figured out how many people will sit along the side, I always add 24 inches to a table's length (2 x 12 inches) to accommodate a person sitting on each end of the table (see the drawing on p. 60).

For round tables, 30 inches is the minimum to allow for each diner, because the eating area is smaller by virtue of being pie-shaped (see the drawing below).

Round table discussion _____

The spaces at a round table get narrower toward the center, so plan on giving each person 30 inches along the table's edge.

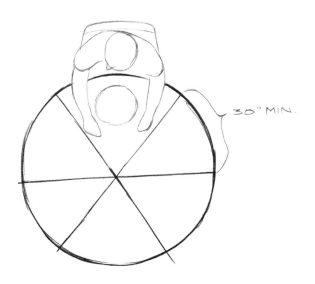

30" MIN.

Avoiding the no man's land

So now you must consider the shape of the top. Round and rectangular are by no means the only options. Square tables are suitable for up to eight people. To seat twelve—three on a side—would require at least a 7-foot square, which leads to a no man's land in the center that no man, woman or beast can reach. The same thing happens with those 8-foot round banquet tables. They're OK at the Waldorf-Astoria, but they don't work if you're serving homestyle. No one can reach to the center of such a table without dragging his tie through the custard. What worked for King Arthur does not necessarily work at home.

Consider the same dilemma when you are deciding dimensions for the width of your table. Most dining tables average about 36 inches across and vary from 30 inches to 48 inches. A narrow table adds intimacy between diners on opposite sides. Anything wider than 4 feet presents that no man's land with the logistical problem of passing the food or reaching the wine.

If 5 feet is the largest permissible square, the smallest comfortable size for a square table for two is about 32 inches; otherwise, knees are bumping, and there is little room for the food. Remember, if you are putting a square or rectangular table in a small area, it is a good idea to round off the corners to prevent bruised thighs when navigating around a table in cramped quarters.

Another popular and traditional form is the oval (or ellipse), which is quite pleasing to the eye. From the builder's perspective, however, it can be difficult. The obstacle is the base: Should it be rectangular or oval? A rectangular base with an oval top looks peculiar when viewed from certain angles. The reason is that the legs are extremely close to the sides, while the end overhang appears disproportionately large (see the bottom drawing on p. 65). It can be a visual disaster, kind of like someone wearing a hat with a too large brim. The alternative is to construct an oval base, not an easy task for the inexperienced.

Think of the room, too

Average chair-seat depth is 16 inches, so it's not surprising that you have to allow at least 36 inches between table edge and wall for someone to push back their chair and stand up. With 44 inches it is even easier to get out of a chair. For wheelchair access, allow 54 inches.

Extension tables leave room for expansion

In those cases where the number of diners will change dramatically from time to time, an extendable table might be the ticket.

There are numerous clever and ingenious methods used to make tables larger and smaller. One of the oldest and simplest methods is the drop-leaf table. One or two sections are hinged and hang down along the table's legs when it's not being used. When the leaves are folded up, a hinged leg or sliding support is moved into position to support the leaves (see the drawing on p. 64).

Like most things in life, drop-leaf tables have their advantages and disadvantages. Because most drop-leaf tables are reduced in size by about two thirds when the leaves are folded down, they work well in places where a table gets occasional use and spends most of its time pushed against a wall. Two disadvantages come to mind: drop-leafs, with their attendant swing-out legs, are not as sturdy as other forms. And when the leaves are folded down against the legs, it is impossible to sit comfortably at the table's side.

A not-too-often seen form of extension table is the swivel top: a rectangular base with a hinged, double rectangular top that swivels 90° and unfolds into a large square (see the top drawing on p. 65).

The most common extension table consists of two halves connected by two telescoping slides onto which one or more leaves are added. Each 24-inch leaf seats an extra person on each side of the leaf. Keep in mind that a 12-inch leaf will not accommodate an additional person. Although I have built scores of different extension tables, I have my reservations about their utility. A table cut in half and rejoined with slides is just not as sturdy as a solid table base.

Three tables can work as one

I have come up with a successful solution to the problem of a varying number of dinner guests. I designed a set of three tables for a family that liked to entertain but did not have the room for one massive table. The main table was 3 feet by 7 feet, with two additional 3-foot square tables that could be

Drop-leaf table saves space

Hinged sections of the top fold up, and the legs swing out to support the leaves. Although they are very versatile, drop-leaf tables are not the most stable table design.

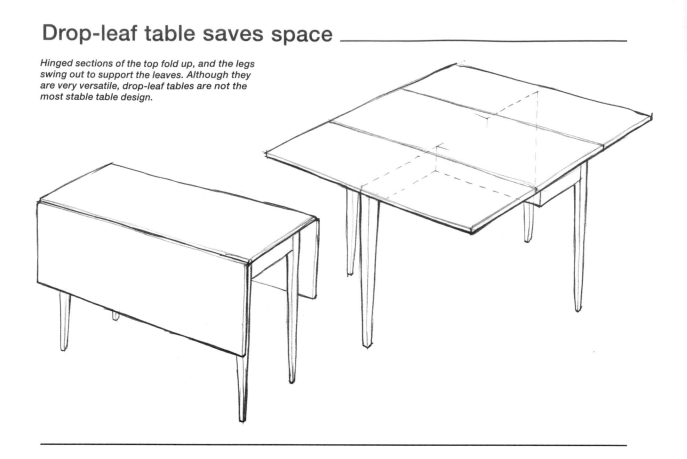

butted against the ends of the main table as the number of dinner guests increased. One of the square tables was used as a side table on a everyday basis, while the other one had folding legs and was stored in the closet. This setup gave them the maximum flexibility of using one, two or three tables, separately or together in any number of configurations.

Table base basics

Once you decide how many people you want to put around your table and determine the shape of your top, you should make sure your diners will not have table legs and aprons bumping into their knees. There are three basic forms of dining table bases (see the top drawing on p. 66).

The pedestal table base has a single leg or grouping of legs in the middle, with cross-bracing on top and a heavy base on the floor

for stability. Because there is usually no apron—there is little structural need for one—the table design allows for additional legroom. Pedestal bases often allow room for crossing legs at the table. The major drawback is the large base, spread out on the floor under the table. No matter how carefully planned, it gets in the way and takes a beating every time diners move their feet.

A good rule of thumb for pedestal tables is that the pedestal's base should cover a footprint just 6 inches smaller in all four directions than the perimeter of the top (see the bottom drawing on p. 66). For instance, a table with a 36-inch by 60-inch top should have a base footprint of 24 inches by 48 inches. Anything more than 6 inches from the perimeter and there's a danger of the table tipping when someone puts weight on the table's edge as they push their chair away and stand up. On a large, heavy table, the pedestal footprint can be up to a foot smaller in each direction than the perimeter of the top because the table's weight will act as a counterbalance.

Trestle tables are similar to pedestal tables in some respects: The feet are subject to wear and tear, and the lack of an apron allows diners to cross their legs while dining. It gets its name from its trestle supports, which are a series of legs (with a foot attached at the bottom) connected by a horizontal beam running the length of the table.

I find that on wide tables a single trestle leg at each end creates too much torque on the upper joints. My solution on tables wider than 36 inches is to use two closely spaced legs on each end.

Trestle tables need at least a 14-inch overhang on each end. A 16- to 18-inch overhang is even better. Without such a long overhang, the trestle will be in the way of end-of-the-table diners' knees (see the top drawing on p. 67).

As common and humble as the four-legged table appears, I believe it is still the best compromise: adequate leg room under the aprons, table legs that shouldn't interfere with diners, and extreme stability. However, leg placement limits chair placement, so it is harder to add more chairs than the number called for in the original design without having one of the diners sit with a leg between his legs. That is why the pedestal table is more popular in many restaurants.

Table height is crucial to comfort

Until about 1950, the normal table height was 29 inches, and antique dining-table tops were 28 inches or even 27 inches high. The population is definitely getting taller, so table height today is usually 30 inches. An exception to this is if you are designing a table to accompany an existing set of chairs. Today's typical chair-seat height is 17 inches. Few things are more disconcerting that eating at a too-high table where your chin is in the soup, so if you are designing a table for a set of low, antique chairs, you might want to consider lowering the table height.

Swivel-top table doubles in size ___

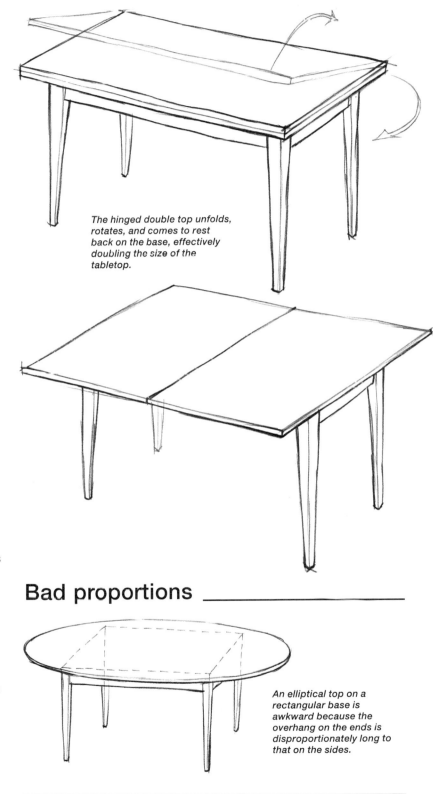

The hinged double top unfolds, rotates, and comes to rest back on the base, effectively doubling the size of the tabletop.

Bad proportions ___

An elliptical top on a rectangular base is awkward because the overhang on the ends is disproportionately long to that on the sides.

It's not just a question of style _____

Pedestal, trestle, and four-legged table bases all have different ergonomic benefits.

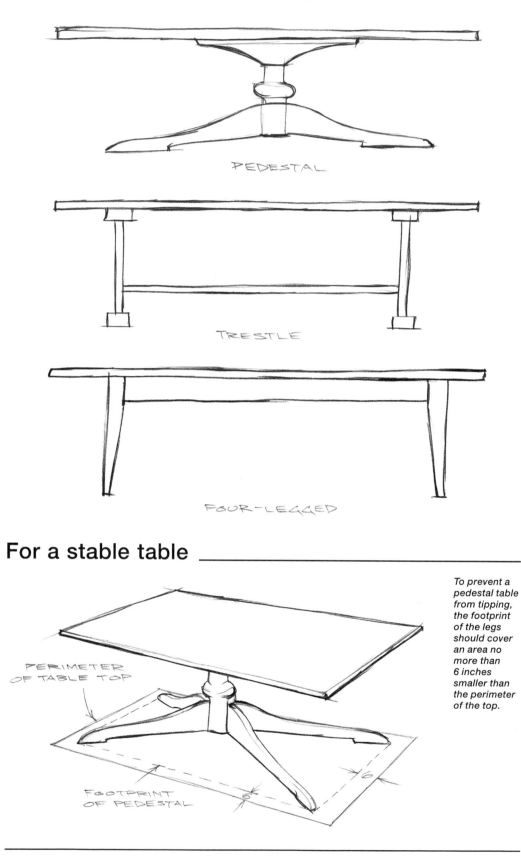

PEDESTAL

TRESTLE

FOUR-LEGGED

For a stable table _____

To prevent a pedestal table from tipping, the footprint of the legs should cover an area no more than 6 inches smaller than the perimeter of the top.

PERIMETER OF TABLE TOP

FOOTPRINT OF PEDESTAL

Need that knee room

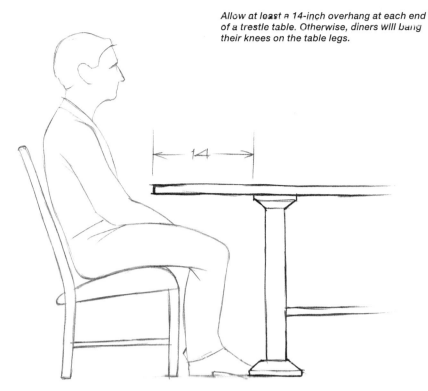

Allow at least a 14-inch overhang at each end of a trestle table. Otherwise, diners will bang their knees on the table legs.

14

Cut away the apron for more knee room

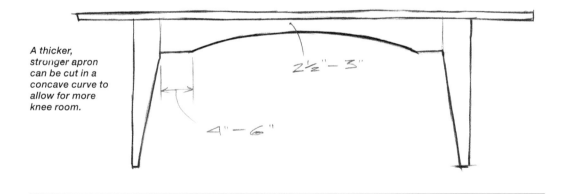

A thicker, stronger apron can be cut in a concave curve to allow for more knee room.

2½" – 3"

4" – 6"

Even with the 30-inch height, today's dining tables don't allow diners to cross their legs—except at trestle tables or pedestal tables without aprons. Even without crossing your legs, you need at least 25 inches of vertical leg room on any table. This means that on a 30-inch-high table with a 1-inch-thick top, you should have no more than a 4-inch apron.

If you think you need a thicker apron for strength, there is a trick that works for me. I make a wider apron—giving me a stronger mortise-and-tenon joint and a more stable table—but I cut the apron smaller for more legroom by starting a concave curve about 4 to 6 inches from the table leg and curving up to a reduced depth of 2½ to 3 inches (see the bottom drawing above).

ENGINEERING A TABLE WITH DRAWERS

by Will Neptune

I like to tell my woodworking students that there's a Shaker nightstand hidden in every table with drawers. I may be overstating my case, but only by a bit. At the North Bennet Street School, we teach strategy. Our largely traditional approach to building tables with drawers isn't the only approach, but it's almost endlessly adaptable; once you understand it, you can apply it to Chippendale writing desks, Pembroke tables, contemporary tables, whatever you like. An approach is liberating: It leaves room for good design and good workmanship while eliminating the need for mock-ups, prototypes and reinventing the wheel.

There's nothing new about this attitude. Thomas Chippendale's Chippendale Director contains page after page of chairs and chair backs. No joints. No dimensions. Nothing about how to build a Chippendale chair. Chippendale assumes his readers already know how to build a chair and that chairs are all built the same way.

When our students build a table with drawers, they learn a system. I recall one student who started a veneered Pembroke table after having done a simpler table with a drawer. "Remember when you built the Shaker nightstand?" I said to him. "Now here's what you're gonna do different." His eyes lit up and he said, "Ah, and you just make this longer, and curve that and, oh, yeah, yeah, yeah." He already knew how to build a Pembroke table—he just didn't realize it.

The single-drawer demonstration table I built (see the photo on the facing page) reveals the basic components of a simple table-with-drawer system: dividers, which replace the front rail to make room for the drawer; doublers, which fill out the side rails and serve as drawer guides; runners, which support the weight of the drawer; and kickers, which keep the drawer from tipping upward when pulled out. Some tables require ledgers to support the runners and kickers, and there are others that do without doublers. Nevertheless, if you took apart a Pembroke table, you'd find the basic components in one fashion or another. And you'd know the secret to building tables with drawers: Inside, they're all about the same. Knowing this is like having a deck full of jokers. You can just keep playing the cards.

A strategy for construction as well as design

It's worth taking a close look at the components that make up the table-with-drawer system, not only in terms of how each functions as part of an overall design but also in terms of how each is constructed in concert with the other components. Although there's no reason why you couldn't apply my strategy to building a table by hand, I'm going to assume you will use a tablesaw and a thickness planer. For me, efficiency demands the use of machines, even for the construction of traditional furniture forms.

The key to efficient construction lies in designing joints that share like dimensions and like locations relative to the leg. The tablesaw cuts related parts to equal length; the planer establishes consistent thicknesses and widths. Together, the tablesaw and thickness planer allow groups of parts to have compatible machine-cut joints. When you plane the dividers to thickness, you can also plane a number of square-dimensioned sticks for runners, kickers and ledgers. If you make the haunched tenons on the rails and the twin tenons on the lower divider the same length and location from the face of the leg, then you can cut all the mortises on a hollow-chisel mortiser with a single fence setting. And you can cut the main shoulders of these joints, as well as the dovetails on the upper divider, without changing the dado height or the fence setting.

Many tables, one approach. The author's students at North Bennet Street School have used his system (mock-up at left) successfully in many styles of tables (above).

69

The essential table with drawer

The author built this mock-up demonstration table to show the basic components that go into a simple table with a drawer.

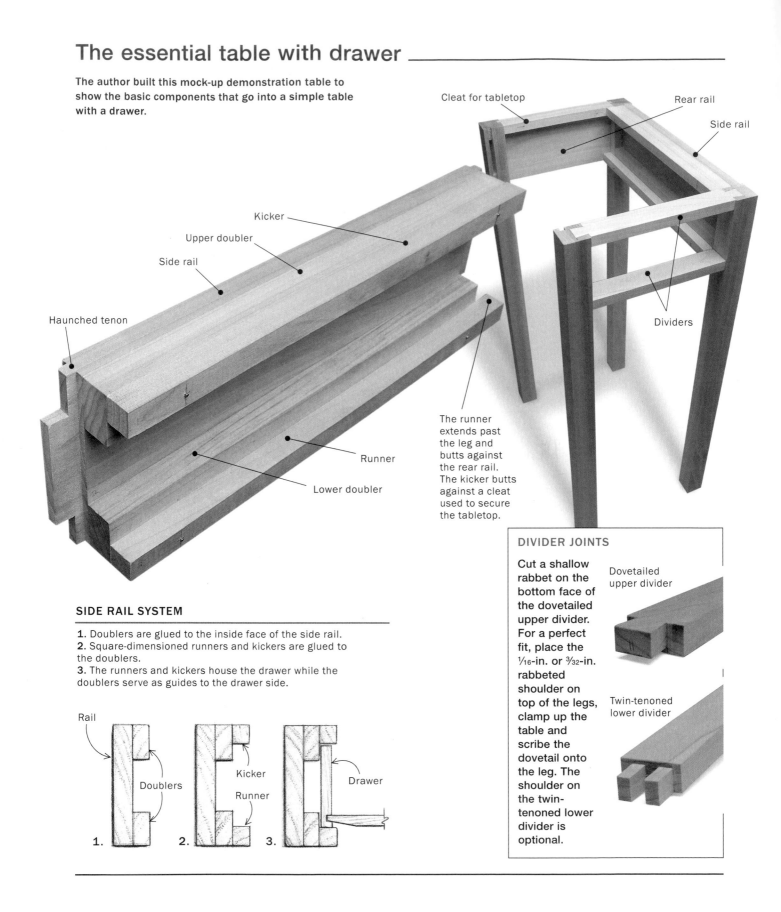

Cleat for tabletop

Rear rail

Side rail

Kicker

Upper doubler

Side rail

Haunched tenon

Dividers

The runner extends past the leg and butts against the rear rail. The kicker butts against a cleat used to secure the tabletop.

Runner

Lower doubler

SIDE RAIL SYSTEM

1. Doublers are glued to the inside face of the side rail.
2. Square-dimensioned runners and kickers are glued to the doublers.
3. The runners and kickers house the drawer while the doublers serve as guides to the drawer side.

Rail

Doublers

Kicker

Runner

Drawer

1.

2.

3.

DIVIDER JOINTS

Cut a shallow rabbet on the bottom face of the dovetailed upper divider. For a perfect fit, place the 1/16-in. or 3/32-in. rabbeted shoulder on top of the legs, clamp up the table and scribe the dovetail onto the leg. The shoulder on the twin-tenoned lower divider is optional.

Dovetailed upper divider

Twin-tenoned lower divider

Once you've milled the pieces, you're ready to put together the essential table: four legs, three rails and two dividers. The upper divider is dovetailed into the leg; the lower divider can't be dovetailed, so it's twin tenoned (see the right drawing on p. 73). With the table glued up, you can take your time installing the inner pieces—doublers, kickers, runners and (if need be) ledgers.

The first pieces to go inside I call doublers because, roughly speaking, they double the thickness of rails. More important, the doublers bring the rail assembly flush to the inside face of the leg, so you don't have to notch the runners and kickers. Some people would call the doublers side guides, and that's what they are as far as the drawer is concerned: blocks that keep the drawer from shifting from side to side as it's pulled out. Cut four doublers to length, and glue them to the top and bottom of the side rails. That's that.

Onto the surface of each doubler, glue one of the little square sticks you thickness planed at the same time as the dividers, one stick at the top of each upper doubler to serve as a kicker, one stick at the bottom of each lower doubler to serve as a runner. Taken together, a doubler and runner or a doubler and kicker form an L-shaped piece of wood, which you could make by rabbeting one piece. But they're much easier to make and install inside the table as two pieces. The wide face of the doublers remains stable when glued flush against the rail. The kickers and runners are such small squares that they won't curl or twist.

What to do when the span gets long

On a small table like my single-drawer demonstration table, gluing the runners and kickers to the doublers, letting them butt against the dividers and the rear rail (or a cleat for securing the tabletop), provides enough strength to support the drawer. On a larger or heftier table or on a table with multiple drawers (see the photo on pp. 72-73), you may need to join the runners and kickers at the front and back of the table. At the front, you can tenon the runners to the lower divider and the kickers to the upper divider. You may not want to tenon the runners and kickers at the back of the table, however, because you'd have to glue up all the pieces at once. Imagine doing that on a five-drawer lowboy with offset drawers!

To avoid having to glue up all those sticks at once, dado two small sticks (which you have milled and ready) across their width to accept a half-lap joint from each runner and kicker, and then brad the sticks temporarily to the rear rail as ledger strips (see the left drawing on p. 73). To allow you to install the kickers and runners after the table frame is glued up, cut them a touch short. Cut the tenons relatively short as well. Even a $^{3}/_{8}$-in. tenon will take the weight of a drawer. Just slide in the tenons, and snap the pieces into place. Then slide in the ledgers, using the brads to locate them for gluing.

If the span of the table is long and you need the dividers to be stronger, there are only two things you can do: Make the dividers wider, or make them thicker. Making them thicker is, by far, the easiest route to take because a little thickness adds a lot of strength. But many designs simply won't allow for a thick divider.

If you settle on making wide dividers, however, you'd better make them really wide. An extra $^{1}/_{2}$ in. of width isn't going to increase the stiffness of the divider to speak of, and an undersized divider will deflect downward. I'd make the divider 4 in. wide at least; a 4-in. divider is no more work than a narrower one. The trouble is, a wide divider stands a good chance of cupping or twisting.

Revealed: A table with multiple drawers

In this demonstration table, the author reveals the components of a long table with multiple drawers. For illustrative purposes, he built two types of partitions.

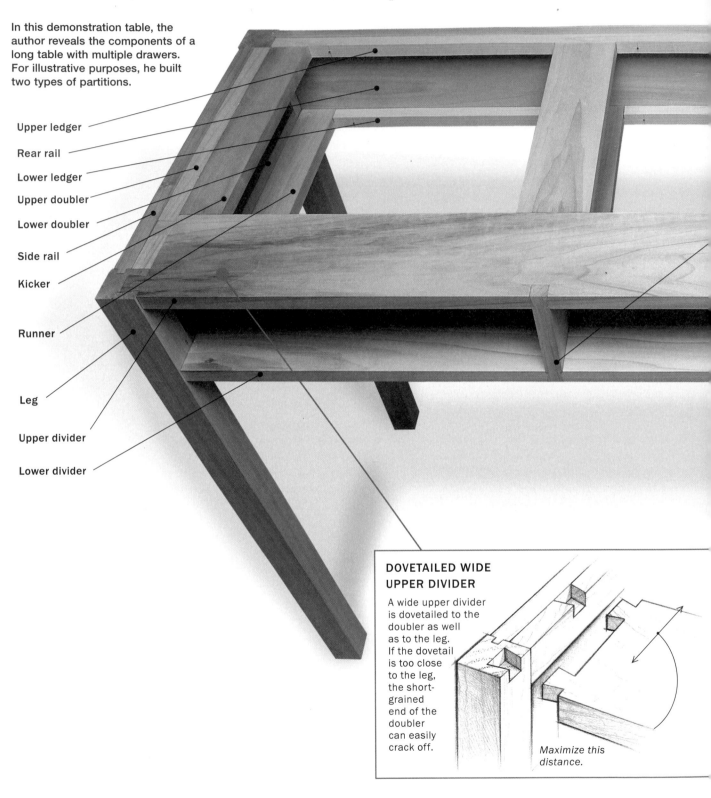

Upper ledger

Rear rail

Lower ledger

Upper doubler

Lower doubler

Side rail

Kicker

Runner

Leg

Upper divider

Lower divider

DOVETAILED WIDE UPPER DIVIDER

A wide upper divider is dovetailed to the doubler as well as to the leg. If the dovetail is too close to the leg, the short-grained end of the doubler can easily crack off.

Maximize this distance.

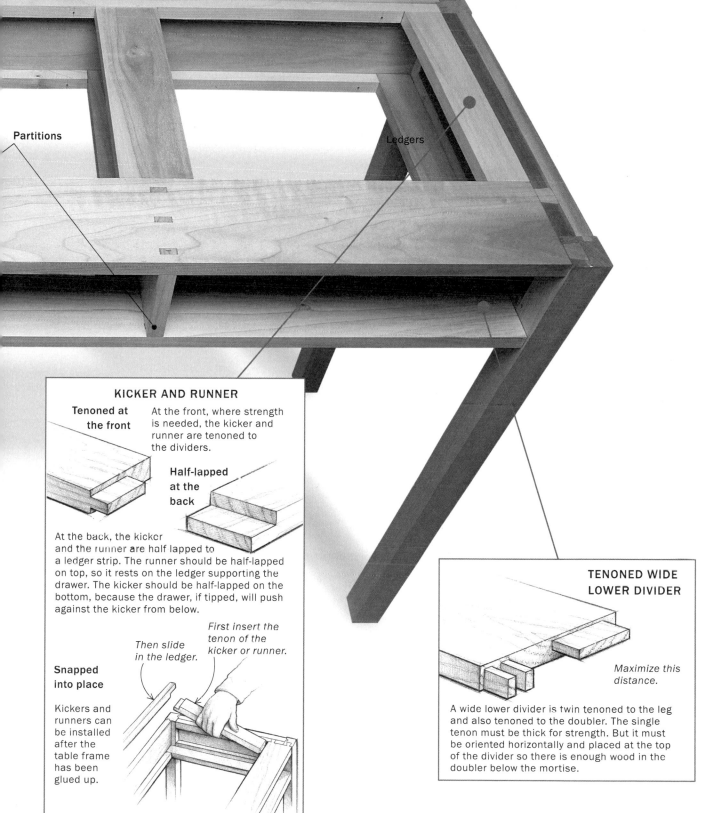

Partitions

Ledgers

KICKER AND RUNNER

Tenoned at the front

At the front, where strength is needed, the kicker and runner are tenoned to the dividers.

Half-lapped at the back

At the back, the kicker and the runner are half lapped to a ledger strip. The runner should be half-lapped on top, so it rests on the ledger supporting the drawer. The kicker should be half-lapped on the bottom, because the drawer, if tipped, will push against the kicker from below.

Then slide in the ledger.

First insert the tenon of the kicker or runner.

Snapped into place

Kickers and runners can be installed after the table frame has been glued up.

TENONED WIDE LOWER DIVIDER

Maximize this distance.

A wide lower divider is twin tenoned to the leg and also tenoned to the doubler. The single tenon must be thick for strength. But it must be oriented horizontally and placed at the top of the divider so there is enough wood in the doubler below the mortise.

Two partition options that support the span

Dovetailed partition

A dovetailed partition is easier to install than a tenoned partition because it can be slipped into place after the dividers have been assembled.

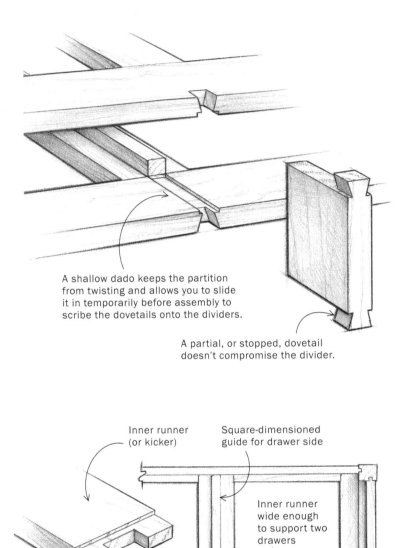

A shallow dado keeps the partition from twisting and allows you to slide it in temporarily before assembly to scribe the dovetails onto the dividers.

A partial, or stopped, dovetail doesn't compromise the divider.

Inner runner (or kicker)

Square-dimensioned guide for drawer side

Inner runner wide enough to support two drawers

Notch the tenon joining the runner (or kicker) to the divider to leave room for the vertical tenons of the partition.

Lower divider

Partition

Tenoned partition

The strongest way to tie together the dividers between the drawers is a vertical partition with through twin tenons or triple tenons. (The plan view drawing below is shown at the lower divider.)

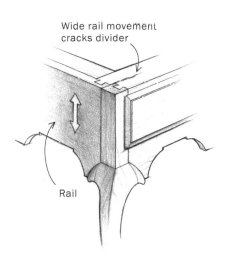

Wide rail movement cracks divider

Rail

To resist racking, you have to join a wide divider not only to the legs but also to either the doublers or the side rails.

When you join a divider to a side rail or doubler, however, you run the risk that the movement of the rail as it expands and contracts will work the divider like a lever. To prevent movement in the rails from cracking the dividers, keep the rails relatively narrow (ideally less than 4 in. wide), and make the dividers really wide so that movement at the inner dovetail is spread out over a greater distance before it reaches the front dovetail.

Joining the dividers directly to the side rails is historically accurate, but it's tricky because you have to mill dividers longer than the rear rail and then notch the dividers around the leg. The other way to join wide dividers—attaching them to the doublers—is awfully tempting. A big advantage to attaching wide dividers to the doublers rather than to the rails is that you can make both dividers the same length as the rear rail. The dovetails are easy to cut because they share a shoulder, and all these shoulders can be cut with the same dado setup used for the rail tenons. The forward dovetail is joined to the leg exactly as it would be on a narrow divider. The inner dovetail can be either a full dovetail, as it is

in my demonstration table, or a half-dovetail. In either case, leave as much space as possible between the inner dovetail and the end of the doubler. If the housing for the dovetail is close to the end of the doubler, the little short-grained piece that remains can easily crack off.

Joining the lower divider to the lower doubler is a little trickier. The lower divider, you remember, is twin tenoned into the leg, so you don't want to dovetail it to the lower doubler because then assembly would be difficult. Instead, join the lower divider to the lower doubler with a horizontal tenon, cut to the same length as the twin tenons. This inner tenon must be as thick as possible for strength, with little or no shoulder on top, so there is enough wood in the doubler below the mortise to provide adequate strength; the doubler will still have plenty of wood above the mortise (see the right drawing on p. 73).

Whether you make the dividers wider or thicker, sizing them is a judgment call. Err on the side of over-built. If the table bounces, what are you going to do about it? If it's a bit sturdier than it needs to be, you'll never know, and you'll be none the worse for it.

How to handle more than one drawer

A table with multiple drawers requires a partition tying together the dividers between each drawer and a complement of internal runners, kickers and drawer guides. It makes sense to mill the partitions at the same time as the dividers; just be sure to leave the divider blanks long, and whack the ends off. There are your partitions, already at the proper width.

If you feel comfortable with the span of the dividers and you simply want two drawers for looks or functionality, then you can stop dado a non-structural partition into the dividers from behind. But if the dividers are really long—for example, 3 ft. or 4 ft.— the stopped-dadoed partition may pop out when the table deflects downward.

The easiest way to strengthen the joint between the partition and the divider is to use the same twin-tenon arrangement used to join the lower divider to the legs. On my multi-drawer demonstration table, the dividers are so wide, I used triple tenons (see the bottom photo and drawing on p. 74), but the idea is the same. I usually run the tenons through the dividers and sometimes even wedge them. If you join a pair of 3-ft. dividers together with two partitions and join the whole assembly to the legs, then you've created a girder. It's amazing how stiff this system is.

So now that you have partitions between the dividers, how do you support the drawers in the middle of the table? You mill runners and kickers wide enough to support drawers on both sides of the partitions, tenon them to the dividers and half-lap them to the ledger on the rear rail.

Treat these inner runners and kickers as you would the runners and kickers next to the doublers, with one big exception. You have to notch the middle of the tenons so they don't interfere with the vertical twin tenons of the partition. To keep the drawers from swimming around, take another square stick, and glue it onto the center of the runner, long grain to long grain, to serve as a drawer-side guide. Problem solved.

You could also dovetail the partition to the dividers. A dovetailed housing cut across the full width of the dividers would compromise the dividers, so use a stopped dovetail in the front to tie the dividers together, plus a shallow 1/8-in. dado across the width of the dividers to keep the partition from twisting (see the top drawing on p. 74).

Dovetailed partitions are easier to install than tenoned partitions because with dovetailed partitions, you can attach both dividers to the legs and then simply slip the partitions into place. The shallow dado allows you to slip the partition into the dividers and then scribe the tail onto the dividers before cutting its housing. It's possible to cut the dado narrower than the dovetail to hide it from the front, but now I'm getting into variations on variations.

The beauty of this approach to engineering a table with drawers is that it doesn't rely on the proportions or the style of the table. You can cut big legs or little legs; you can set the rails flush to the legs or inset them; you can turn the legs or taper them; you can make the table long and low and turn it into a coffee table or tall and long and call it a writing desk.

What I hope I've constructed here is a conceptual framework onto which you can overlay your own design ideas.

ATTACHING TABLETOPS

by Garrett Hack

I've repaired quite a few antiques, many of them tables with cracked tops. And the reason for the crack is always the same: The top had been attached to the base without any allowance for the wood to move.

Properly attached, a tabletop can expand and contract with changes in humidity while staying flat and firmly connected to its base.

Tables that are properly connected gain strength from their connections, the top lending rigidity to the base and the base reinforcing the top.

Of the five common methods of connecting tabletops to their bases covered here, four of them are shopmade and one of them relies on commercially available metal clips.

Simple fixture accurately positions rail for boring pocket holes. The author's fixture consists of a length of softwood, its face angled at 10°, screwed to a plywood base.

A good connection for period furniture. A V-shaped cut on the inside of a table rail seats the screw attaching the top and is a nice visual touch.

Pocket holes are great for small tables. But because they allow so little cross-grain wood movement, they're not well-suited to tables with wide tops.

Three-faceted pocket holes can be made quickly with a sharp chisel and some practice. The V-shaped hole provides a good seat for the screw head.

Screw blocks make a secure connection. Glued to the rail and screwed to the underside of the tabletop, screw blocks can be attached after the whole base is finished.

Which of these methods is appropriate depends on the size of your table, its construction and, perhaps most important, on your tastes and preferences. Each has its place and, in some instances, a combination of them may be the best solution.

By the way, these methods have applications beyond connecting tabletops to bases. They're just as useful for attaching tops to chests of drawers, desks and other case pieces.

Accounting for wood movement

Wood moves. Sometimes it moves a lot. Most of the expansion and contraction takes place across the grain, whether the boards have been flatsawn or quartersawn. On average, quartersawn wood moves a little less than half as much as flatsawn. Wood hardly moves at all in length. (For a good discussion of wood movement and other properties of wood, see *Understanding Wood: A Craftsman's Guide to Wood Technology* by R. Bruce Hoadley, The Taunton Press, 1980.)

If you're making a leg-and-apron table with a solid-wood top, this means that you have to allow the top to move independently of the base. On small tables (say, 18 in. or less in a relatively stable wood, like cherry), the movement of the top is slight and can almost be ignored. On wider tables, however, you need to allow for some significant movement—especially if you live in a part of the country with big swings in humidity.

To help me gauge how much movement I can expect, I keep a few short, wide boards around. Every three weeks or so, I'll mark the date and width of these boards right on the boards. This gives me a running record of actual wood movement (not theoretical movement) in my part of the country on some of the species that I use most often. I've been doing this for a few years now, so I have a pretty good idea of how much movement to allow for when I build a piece.

For the sake of clarity, I'll explain these attachment methods on a simple table of legs and rails, but the methods work just as well on more complex structures with inter-

nal cross rails or strongbacks. I often use more than one kind of attachment on the same piece, taking advantage of each method's strengths to suit my particular design.

Whichever method I choose, I attach the top to the side rails (the side perpendicular to the grain in the top) every 4 in. to 8 in., starting quite close to the leg. For the front and back rails, I generally use only about half as many attachments. That's because the movement in most rectangular tops is across the grain, front to back. By attaching the top at more points along the side rails, I can keep the top from curling or cupping. Fewer attachments at front and rear mean that those rails can bow slightly, if necessary, as the top moves with seasonal changes in humidity.

Pocket holes: a simple solution for small tables

Pocket holes are holes bored at an angle, usually about 10°, through a rail for a screw that connects the base and the top (see the top photo on the facing page). Actually, two holes are drilled. One provides a seat for the screw head, and the other, a pilot hole, prevents the screw from splitting the rail or the top.

Pocket holes are easy to make and provide a positive connection between top and base. Their biggest liability is that they don't allow the top to move much. Pocket holes are best suited to smaller or shallower tables where the top isn't wide enough to produce much movement.

Pocket holes can be made to allow for more movement by drilling slightly oversized pilot holes or by making the holes oval in the direction of movement. I use a small round or rat-tail file to do this. I often attach the front edge of a top securely with a couple of screws through pocket holes and then progressively enlarge the screw holes the farther away from the front rail I go. On other table designs, where I want the movement roughly equal on either side of the center of the top, I fix the top securely in

Wooden buttons look nice and are simple to make. They also allow for a good deal of movement. To ensure the buttons won't break, make sure that their grain runs perpendicular to the rails.

Dovetail blocks allow the most movement but are the hardest to make. Screws attach the pin block to the underside of the table; the slot block is glued to the side of the table, just like a screw block.

the middle of the two short rails. Half the movement of the top will be toward the front of the table, the other half toward the back.

Another drawback to using pocket holes on wider tabletops is that oversizing or "ovalizing" the screw holes in the back rail can be quite time-consuming and will weaken the back rail as well. The rail can be strengthened by gluing another rail to it, or you can avoid the problem altogether by just using another kind of connector here.

On shallow tables with long rails, I have sunk one or more screws through pocket holes in the back rail, well away from the legs. This allows the rail to bow in and out slightly with the changes in humidity.

I usually drill my pocket holes on the drill press, using a simple fixture that positions the rail at about 10° off vertical (see the inset photo on p. 77). I drill the pocket with a Forstner bit and then follow up by drilling the screw hole with a twist bit of appropriate size. You can buy bits that do both operations simultaneously, but they don't do the job as cleanly.

For a nice touch, especially on a period table, the seat for the screw head can be cut with a chisel by making a V-shaped cut into the apron at an angle and leaving a small flat at the bottom for the screw head (see the left photo on p. 77 and the center photo on p. 78). First efforts aren't usually great, but you'll get it down if you do a few trial cuts on a piece of scrap.

Screw blocks: quick and convenient

Screw blocks are small blocks of wood glued to the rails, flush with the upper edge, and then screwed to the top (see the bottom photo on p. 78). They work like pocket holes, so on wider tabletops, the hole through the block should be oval on the side of the block against the top. Screw blocks, like pocket holes, make very secure connections.

One of the main advantages of using screw blocks is that they can be made, fitted and installed near the end of the construction process; most of the other methods require that you either drill or mortise the rails before gluing up the base.

Screw blocks sometimes work in situations where drilling pocket holes is awkward or impossible—for example, where a large drawer fills most of the space between rails. Screw blocks actually can strengthen the whole structure if they're glued between the drawer guides and the table's rails. I've used screw blocks successfully with extension tables by placing them between the rails and extension slides.

Also, screw blocks can allow greater movement than pocket holes. To do that, cut a slot all the way through the blocks in the direction of wood movement in the top, and use a round-head screw and steel washer instead of a bugle-head-style screw. With their holes elongated, screw blocks are useful for wider tops that move a lot seasonally.

Buttons: elegant solution for tables large and small

Buttons are small blocks of wood tenoned on one side of one end, creating a half-lap joint that engages a slot cut into the rail. The buttons are screwed to the tabletop (see the top photo on the facing page).

Buttons are my preferred method of attaching tabletops because they're easy to make and install. They work well in many situations, and they make a secure connection. Their major advantage over other methods is that they allow a lot of movement in two directions, both along the rail and perpendicular to it. I avoid using them only when there is too little space, such as where a drawer uses the back rail as its stop.

When I use buttons, I locate and fix the top either at the front edge or in the center, depending on what kind of table it is, using a pocket hole or screw block. This helps me control where the seasonal movement of the wood will occur.

Buttons can be made from most any hardwood, but maple, birch and ash are my favorites because of their strength. I cut the tenons on buttons to roughly half the button's thickness and about $1/4$ in. to $3/8$ in.

long. Overall, the buttons are approximately ³/₄ in. thick, 1 in. wide and 1¹/₂ in. to 2 in. long, with the grain running the button's length.

I cut the button mortises in the rails before assembling the base, either by hand with chisels or, more often, with a slot mortiser. You also could use a plunge router or cut the slot mortises after assembly with a router and bearing-guided slotting bit by running the router along the top of the rail. This method works particularly well on curved rails because it lets you cut the mortises after the leg-and-rail assembly has been leveled and trued.

I position the mortises slightly lower on the rail than the space between the top of the button and the top of the half lap would indicate. This causes the buttons to fall slightly below the top of the rail so that when the buttons are screwed to the top, the connection is very tight. I've seen buttons engage a groove the length of the rail, but this can weaken the table. I also keep the buttons slightly away from the legs, so the leg-to-rail joint won't be weakened.

If I've secured the tabletop at the front so that all movement is to the back of the table, I make the mortises in the rear rail slightly deeper and the corresponding tenons slightly longer than those on the sides. Then I position the shoulders of the buttons' half laps away from the rail a bit, and I take care not to seat the end of the buttons' tenons. This allows for more movement where it's most needed.

Dovetail blocks: best method for lots of movement

Dovetail blocks are two-part connectors. A dovetail-shaped piece is screwed to the top, and a block with a corresponding slot is glued to the rail (see the bottom photos on p. 80). Their primary advantage over other methods is that they allow for a great deal of wood movement, making them best suited to wide tops on tables with straight rails.

They're fairly time-consuming to cut, fit and install, but they work well and make a good connection.

When I cut dovetail blocks, I make sure I have a good fit between the pin blocks and slot blocks. The blocks shouldn't bind or be sloppy. I cut the slot on a router table and then cut the stock into 2-in.- to 3-in.-long pieces. I rip the pin blocks slightly oversize on the tablesaw and then handplane them to get a perfect fit. I secure these blocks to the top with two screws and then glue the slot blocks to the side rails. For the front and back rails, the slot blocks are mortised into the rails or another type of connector is used, such as screw blocks or buttons.

Metal fasteners: simple, not elegant

Two types of metal fasteners are widely available. One is a figure-eight style (see the bottom photos on the facing page), and the other is a clip that looks like a squared-up "Z" (see the top photo on the facing page). Both fasteners are inexpensive, easy to install and plenty strong for most applications.

The Z-clip functions exactly like a wooden button, with one offset let into a sawkerf near the top of the rail and the other screwed to the top. These clips allow for a great deal of wood movement. My only problem with using them is aesthetic: I just don't think they belong on fine furniture. I prefer using the more elegant shopmade buttons on any but the most utilitarian projects.

For the figure-eight style, one part of the "8" is set flush into a hole drilled with a flat-bottomed bit in the top of the rail, with the center of the fastener just out from the rail. The other end is screwed to the top. This allows the clip to rotate through a small arc to accommodate wood movement. One advantage of using these connectors is that you can install them late in the construction process. They're best suited to modest-sized tables because of their limited range of movement.

Metal fasteners are inexpensive and easy to install. All you need to do is slot your rails. The clips allow for plenty of movement in all but the largest tables, but they don't have a refined look.

Figure-eight clips can be installed after the base is complete. With these clips, you drill only one shallow, flat-bottomed hole in the rail. Screw the other half of the "8" into the underside of the tabletop.

BREADBOARD ENDS TO KEEP TOPS FLAT

by Garrett Hack

Good breadboard ends allow seasonal wood movement while keeping a tabletop flat. The battens on the top of the author's cherry dining-room table are mortised to receive four separate tenons at each end of the table. Rosewood pins add strength and visual interest.

Sooner or later every woodworker has to come to terms with breadboard ends. You can reject them as nonessential elements, or you can reject them just because they take time and effort to make and attach. But if you want an elegantly practical way to keep desktops, tabletops, chest lids and other panels flat, adding breadboard ends is the way to go.

But what are breadboard ends (sometimes, they are called just breadboards) anyway? Basically, a breadboard is just a narrow

board (or batten) at the end of and running cross-grain to a panel, preventing the panel from cupping. To attach the breadboard to the panel, you need a joint that keeps the end snug to the end grain of the top. The joint must be strong enough not to break off (even if the panel is picked up by the breadboard end itself), yet it still must allow the top to expand and contract with seasonal changes in humidity.

Fortunately, there are a number of useful joints for attaching breadboard ends, ranging from crude but functional to fine and elegant, though more time-consuming, solutions. All share a tongue and groove or sliding dovetail, either of which will keep the batten and panel engaged over the whole length of the batten.

In deciding which technique to use for a particular application, I consider the end use of the item, the type(s) of wood in which I'm cutting the joint, the width of the panel being breadboarded, how wide the batten should be (both structurally and aesthetically) and how the breadboards relate to the overall design. For example, the breadboards for a cutting board don't need to be as fancy as those for a drop-front on a traditional desk. Similarly, the lid to a small writing box won't be subject to the rigors a dining-room table will be, so the simplest solution that's in keeping with the design of such a piece is probably best. Also, the wider the batten, the more stiffness it can impart, but the trade-off is that it's also more vulnerable to being broken off.

There's one final aesthetic consideration: Because the panel will be moving across its width with fluctuations in humidity, the outside edges of the table and the breadboard will rarely line up flush. Part of the year, the breadboard will project past the table edges slightly; at other times, the table edge will be proud. Some people find this objectionable and probably avoid breadboards because of it, but sitting at my

Simple breadboarding techniques

Grooves are cut with the grain in the batten to take advantage of the long-grained strength of the tongue or dovetail in the panel. Spline should have long grain running with the panel.

SPLINED

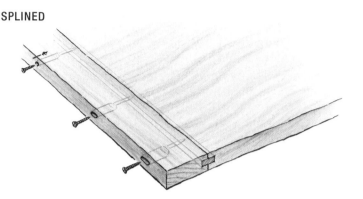

Grooving the panel and the batten and inserting a spline is the simplest way to breadboard an end. Elongated screw holes allow the panel to move.

TONGUE AND GROOVED

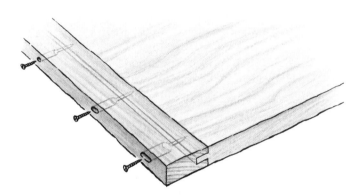

Grooving the batten and rabbeting the panel on both sides to create a tongue take a little more effort, but the joint is stronger and looks nicer.

DOVETAILED

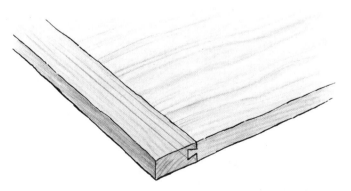

Dovetailing the panel and routing a dovetailed groove in the batten provide mechanical strength to the construction. This joint looks nicer still, but the process requires greater precision.

favorite table, I often find my fingers seeking out this difference, as if to affirm the living nature of wood. I do take care, however, to keep the difference as consistent as possible from side to side, and I slightly ease any sharp edges at the batten ends.

Quick, simple breadboarding

For utilitarian purposes, and even for smaller items you want to make look nice, there are some quick and simple methods of attaching breadboard ends. These basic methods include splining batten and panel together; tongue and grooving the panel end and one edge of the batten; and dovetailing batten and end together (see the drawing at left).

If I'm using well-seasoned, dry stock, I generally feel pretty comfortable gluing the center third of the batten to the top, as long as the panel is less than, say, 30 in. For splined or tongue-and-grooved breadboard ends, I like to use at least two screws on either side of the glued center, one of them a few inches from each edge and one more centered on each side between the outboard screws and the inner pair (see the drawing at left). The outer screws should have elongated holes to allow for at least $1/8$ in. of movement. For the screws closer to the center, I usually just drill slightly oversized holes.

You could also simply nail the batten on. The lids of many old blanket chests feature this construction using cut nails, which hold well in end grain and are less prone to splitting the panel than contemporary wire nails. And cut nails just look nice on more utilitarian, traditional pieces. Cut nails are still available from Tremont Nail Co., which has been making cut nails since 1819 (P.O. Box 111, Wareham, Mass. 02571; 508-295-0038). You wouldn't use this technique for fine work, but it works well for tops that are less than 20 in. or so and for softer woods. It is perfectly satisfactory where function is the sole criterion.

A sliding dovetail between batten and top is a good method for breadboarding smaller surfaces such as cutting boards and, if done well, can be strong and attractive. To work effectively, though, the joint must be tight over its whole length, and this is difficult to do over wide expanses. That's because wide panels tend to cup or warp, causing slight variations in thickness of the dovetail when you rout it, which causes the joint to be either sloppy or too tight in places.

Another drawback is the batten is potentially weakened by the dovetail: The dovetail flares in thickness, requiring that the walls of the batten around the dovetail slot be thinner than they would be for a tongue-and-grooved batten. This situation worsens with thinner stock. For these reasons, when using a sliding-dovetail batten, I keep the batten narrow, making it less liable to be broken off. I also drill and drive a wooden pin or two through the joint at the center of a dovetail batten to keep the movement even on both sides.

The best breadboard: separate tenons, stub tongue

The breadboarding technique I turn to most often is a series of mortise and tenons and a stub tongue and matching groove (see the drawing on p. 88). It's not overly complicated, but it's certainly more time-consuming than the other methods that I have described. It more than makes up for that, though, with its strength, durability and clean appearance. Large separate tenons lend strength and rigidity to the batten ends, helping them withstand being leaned on, lifted (so that they're supporting the entire weight of the table) and all the rest that a kitchen or dining table must endure. The stub tongue keeps top and batten aligned. Pinned, slotted holes in the outer tenons let the panel move while keeping batten ends tight against the panel.

After gluing up the top slightly wide and a couple of inches long, I handplane top and bottom flat, paying particular attention to the two ends where the battens will be attached. Then I square up the top on my bandsaw and jointer, or when working a very large panel, I'll use a handsaw and plane. I mill the battens at the same time, a couple of inches longer than needed and about $1/16$ in. thicker than the table. After the joint has been assembled, I'll plane the

Mortising and grooving the batten ends

A horizontal slot mortiser does a quick, accurate job of mortising the battens. A router and mortising jig or drill press used with a fence would give you similar results.

Cutting a groove in a batten is best done on the tablesaw. You can take multiple cuts with a standard blade, or you can shim a dado to get the proper-thicknessed groove.

Squaring to the mortise layout lines takes just a couple of minutes with a sharp chisel and a mallet.

Mortised-and-tenoned breadboard technique

Using separate tenons for strength and a stub tenon for alignment is the strongest and most durable way of breadboarding.

Two center tenons are glued and pinned in two places. Movement over approximately 1 ft. is insignificant.

Two end tenons have elongated holes and are not glued. This allows unrestricted movement of the tabletop.

Stub tenon ensures alignment of batten and panel (a tabletop in this case) and keeps the tabletop from warping between the four separate tenons.

I always allow for both expansion and contraction, even if it's the end of the dry season and the wood is dry. At the opposite end of the moisture extreme, in more humid months, I'll allow for a bit of expansion, but mostly I plan for the inevitable shrinkage.

Mortising and grooving the batten ends

I cut the batten mortises on a horizontal slot mortiser, and then I square them to my layout lines with a paring chisel (see the top and bottom photos on p. 87). You could also do the mortises with a plunge router, on the drill press or even chop them entirely by hand.

Next I rip the groove that mates with the stub tongue on the tablesaw (see the center photo on p. 87). It's the same width as the mortises. There are times when, for aesthetic reasons, I prefer to have this tongue and groove blind at the outside edges of the table. In those instances, I stop the groove just short of each end by at least $1/4$ in. and mate it to a small haunch cut on the ends of the tongue.

Cutting the tenons and stub tongue

For the tenons, the first thing I do is rout the tenon and tongue areas down to thickness while leaving the stock between the tenons to support the base of the router (see the top photo on the facing page). For the final router pass, I move the fence back ever so slightly to rout a crisp shoulder for the batten to snug up to. Then I do the same on the other side. I take care not to flip the board I'm using for a fence so that any slight deviation in the fence is exactly the same on both sides of the table. Also, it's critical to have both shoulders at exactly the same distance from the tenon ends. I ensure this by making a mark with my knife on either side of the table where the fence meets it and then squaring down from there to the underside of the table.

I square across the tenon stock from the layout lines on both the top and bottom of the table, and then I cut the cheeks with a backsaw and remove the waste with a coping saw (see the center photo on the facing page). I find or plane a small block of scrap to the same thickness as the tongue height and scribe all along the tongue to give me a

whole assembly flat. Other woodworkers may choose to sand the top flat instead.

I mark out the tenons and the shoulder line for the batten on the top, using four tenons evenly spaced, with the outer two starting about 2 in. from the outer edge ($2^1/2$-in.-wide tenons seem to work well). I make them as deep as possible to resist the bending stresses on the batten ends, usually stopping them just about $1/4$ in. from the outside edge of the battens. If the battens will be shaped later, though, I reduce the length of the tenons and the depth of the mortise, so I don't expose the tenons when shaping the batten.

I transfer the layout marks from table to batten, and I mark the tabletop's outer edges on the batten. In my experience, a cherry top of this size, made from straight-grained, not quartersawn, air-dried boards, will move seasonally about $1/4$ in. To compensate for this in the joinery, I mark out mortises about $1/8$ in. wider than the outside tenons and about $1/16$ in. wider than the pair of center tenons.

line to which I can pare and plane. Starting on the back, I use a large paring chisel and then a sharp rabbet plane to true up the tenon cheeks and tongue and just ease the arris (see the bottom photo). I fit the tenons and tongue in the top to the mortises, and I groove in the batten with careful passes with rabbet and block planes until the batten fits snugly over its whole length. A scrap with the batten groove ripped in it is useful to size the tenons and tongue. The extra inch or so of waste at either end of the batten is also helpful for tapping on to remove the batten as you're test-fitting.

Attaching the battens

The pair of center tenons will be glued and pegged into their mortises, but the only thing holding the batten to the table at the outside tenons are small pins, which I draw-bore slightly and drive through elongated holes in the tenons to allow for wood movement. Drawboring simply means that I drill the hole in the tenon just a hair closer to the shoulder than the hole I drill in the batten. This causes the joint to "draw" up tightly when the pins are driven home.

I first drill all of the pin holes through the batten, separate from the table. I use a scrap the same thickness as the tenons inserted in each mortise to prevent tearout. I reassemble the joint, mark pin locations and remove the batten one last time. The holes in the outside tenons need to be slightly closer to the shoulder than the layout marks I transferred from the batten. They need to be elongated, so I use a scrap block of the appropriate thickness as a spacer to mark them. Then I drill all the pin holes and elongate the holes in the outer tenons with a small chisel or gouge.

Next I put a thin layer of glue on the inner tenons, clamp the whole assembly together and then drive the pins home. I like to use a hardwood, such as rosewood, for the pins so that they can be kept small and still work well. After the glue has cured, I'll cut the extra stock off the ends of the battens, trim the pegs nearly flush with the batten and then finish-plane the whole tabletop flat and smooth.

Cutting the tenons and stub tongue

Waste stock between tenons supports the router base. A series of passes with the router takes tenons to thickness.

Horizontal coping-saw cuts remove waste between tenons after vertical backsaw cuts define tenon edges.

Pare the tongue to the line. Use a sharp chisel between the tenons to clean up where the waste was sawed away.

SUPPORTING DROP LEAVES

by Christian H. Becksvoort

A sagging leaf on a drop-leaf table can be a chronic nuisance, to say nothing of the Christmas turkey that could end up in your lap. I've come to rely on six different support systems to keep leaves solidly in place. My favorite is a smooth-acting, pull-out slide that can be sized appropriately for end tables or dining tables. The pull-out slide's simple appearance and operation complements the Shaker-style furniture that I prefer. But no matter what system you choose to support table leaves, you have to hinge the leaves to the table. Let's take a look at the best way to accomplish that.

Drop leaves require a special joint and hinge

The earliest examples of drop-leaf tables tended to be rather sturdy and often had but one leaf. These primitive tables had butt joints between the top and leaf and used plain butt hinges, as shown in the top left drawing on p. 93. A better way is to cut a rule joint where the leaf meets the tabletop, and use a special hinge made specifically for the job.

Drop-leaf hinges, as shown in the bottom drawing on p. 93, have the barrel on one side and the screw countersinks on the other. One leaf of the hinge is longer than the other to span the gap at the edge of the leaf created by the rule joint.

The rule joint consists of a quarter-round with a fillet along the edge of the top and a cove along the edge of the leaf. The rule joint provides a smooth transition from top to leaf, whether the leaf is in the up or down position. It also discourages crumbs, tablecloths and fingers from becoming caught in the closing joint.

Six different support systems

Each of the six support systems has advantages for particular applications. Spinners (see the top left drawing on p. 92) are compact, uncomplicated and work well with smaller leaves, such as those on side tables. Swing arms (see the center drawing on p. 92) also are best for small, light leaves. Swing legs (see the bottom drawing on p. 92) and gate legs (see the top right drawing on p. 92) can be used for smaller leaves but are best for heavy loads, such as dining table extensions, because they transfer loads directly to the floor.

Swing and crane supports (see the right drawing on p. 93) are a compromise between swing arms and swing legs. Because the load of the leaf is distributed between the table's rail and stretcher, these supports will hold more weight than swing arms. But swing and crane supports lack the solid support gained by the swing legs' contact with the floor.

Sliding supports (see the drawing on p. 95) can be proportioned to work well with small, light leaves or leaves that must support heavier loads, as long as the leaf is restricted to half the width of the tabletop.

Spinners

A spinner is basically a stick that pivots on top of the table's side rail to support the leaf. Because only half the overall length of a spinner supports the leaf, it should be as close to twice the width of the leaf as table width and rail length permit. For example, a 10-in. leaf should have about an 18-in. spinner. Half the spinner supports the leaf while the other bears against the underside of the tabletop.

You make spinners right along with the rails. Just start with stock that's a little longer and a little wider than the finished rail. Rip a 1-in.- to 1½-in.-wide strip from the top edge. Then crosscut the strip at 45° to create the spinners, as shown in the top left drawing on p. 92. The 45° cuts let the spinners rotate in only one direction and create positive stops when the spinners are closed.

Glue the pieces that were between and on the ends of the spinners back onto the rail, using the spinners as spacers. On the drill press, drill a ¼-in.-dia. hole through the center of each spinner. Then clamp the spinners into position on top of the rail, and drill through the spinners and into the rail about 1 in. Remove the spinners, and glue a ¼-in.-dia. dowel about 2 in. long into the rail. Redrill the spinners' holes about ¹/₆₄ in. larger than the dowel, so the spinners will rotate freely on the dowel. After the rails are cut to length and width, tenoned and sanded, slide the spinners over the dowels, and trim off any excess dowel length. After the table is completed, glue a

There's more than one way to support a drop leaf. This table uses sliding supports, the author's favorite option, but there are other choices.

Spinner leaf supports

Spinner supports are quick to make and easy to install on table rails without a lot of extra work.

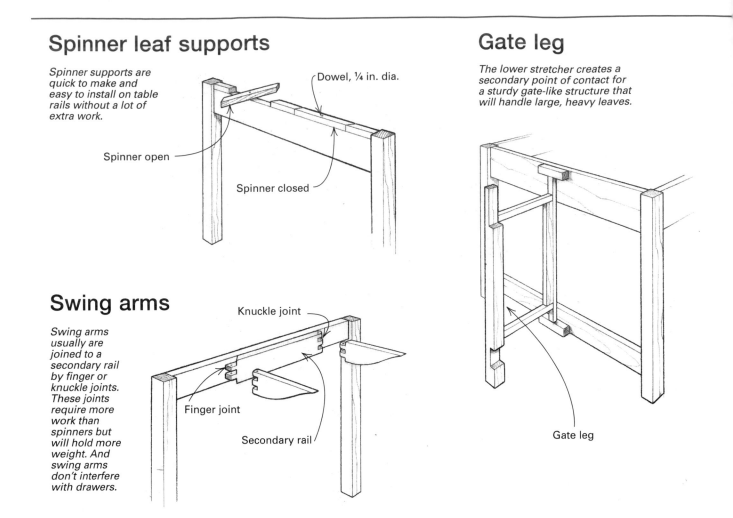

Spinner open

Spinner closed

Dowel, ¼ in. dia.

Gate leg

The lower stretcher creates a secondary point of contact for a sturdy gate-like structure that will handle large, heavy leaves.

Gate leg

Swing arms

Swing arms usually are joined to a secondary rail by finger or knuckle joints. These joints require more work than spinners but will hold more weight. And swing arms don't interfere with drawers.

Knuckle joint

Finger joint

Secondary rail

Swing legs

By transferring the load directly to the floor, swing legs can handle more weight than swing supports.

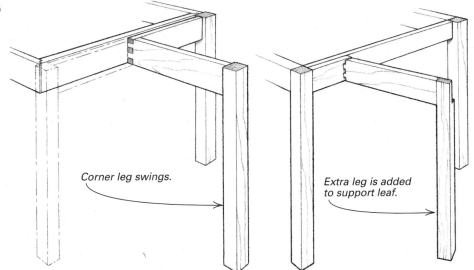

Corner leg swings.

Extra leg is added to support leaf.

Standard hinge

A standard hinge leaves an awkward stepped gap between table and leaf when leaf is in the down position.

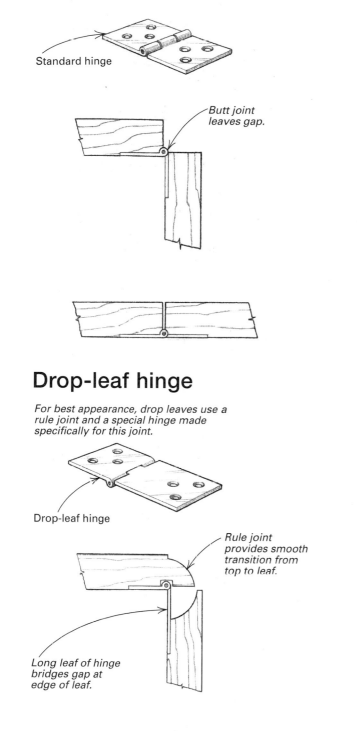

Standard hinge

Butt joint leaves gap.

Drop-leaf hinge

For best appearance, drop leaves use a rule joint and a special hinge made specifically for this joint.

Drop-leaf hinge

Rule joint provides smooth transition from top to leaf.

Long leaf of hinge bridges gap at edge of leaf.

Swing and crane supports

A swing support can handle heavy leaves because of the triangulated weight distribution. A swing support is easy to add to a table.

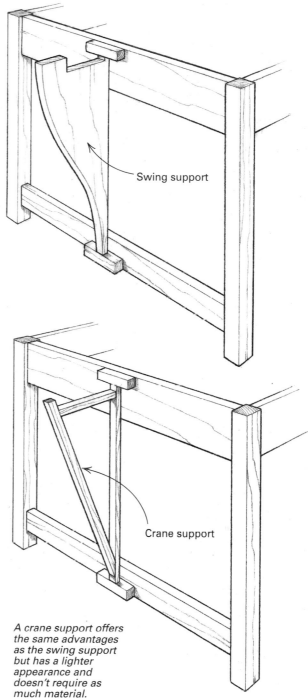

Swing support

Crane support

A crane support offers the same advantages as the swing support but has a lighter appearance and doesn't require as much material.

A sliding drop-leaf support is a neat, clean installation. It provides firm support that won't sag with use. The ⅜-in.-long finger pull at the support's end is all that protrudes when fully retracted.

Housings protect the sliding supports from damage or interference by the drawer's contents. The housings drop into mortises in the drawer kickers. Nylon bumpers make for smooth sliding action.

small block to the underside of the tabletop to stop the spinners at 90° to the rail in the open position.

Swing arms

Swing arms are braces attached to a table's rail that pivot 90° to the rail to support leaves. Swing arms are usually built as part of a secondary rail assembly that is applied to the outside face of the table's side rails. Swing arms are fastened to the secondary rail with either finger joints or knuckle joints, as shown in the center drawing on p. 92.

Finger joints are probably more common because they are easier to cut. Their interlocking parts are square-cornered like a box joint instead of rounded as in a knuckle joint. If you use a finger joint, undercut between the fingers, and round off the inside corner of each finger for clearance. After cutting the joint, slide the pieces together, and drill a hole for a pivot pin. The end of the support can be shaped as desired, but traditionally, it has an ogee shape.

Swing legs

A variation of the swing arm is the swing leg. As with the swing arm, one end of the support arm is joined to a secondary rail by finger joints or knuckle joints. However, the arm portion of the support is usually longer, and rather than being free, the opposite end of the arm is tenoned into its own leg. A variety of leg configurations is possible with swing legs, as shown in the bottom drawings on p. 92. Because of their direct contact to the floor, swing legs can handle heavier leaves than swing arms.

Gate legs

A permutation of the swing leg is the gate leg. If the drop-leaf table has lower stretchers between the legs, then the swinging legs also can include a lower stretcher for a two-point attachment at the top rail and at the bottom stretcher. This gate-like assembly, as shown in the top right drawing on p. 92, is a sturdy support that can handle large, heavy leaves without racking. A gate leg

Sliding drop-leaf supports _____

Slides that support table leaves fit together in a housing when not in use. Supports should be sized according to the size and weight of the leaves. These are suitable for leaves measuring 10 in. by 32 in.

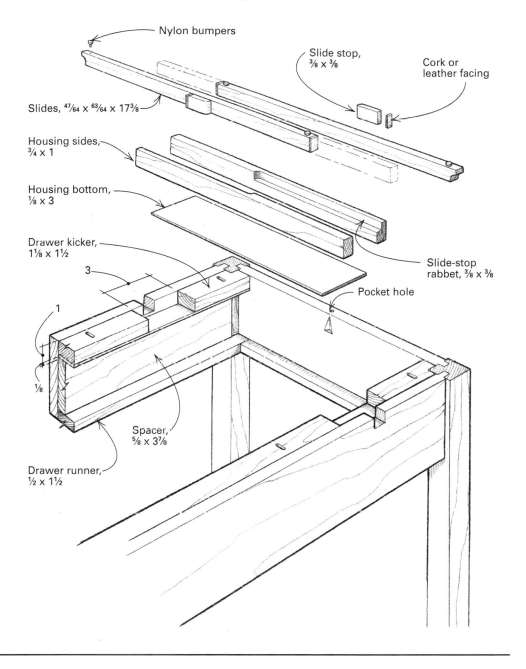

Nylon bumpers

Slide stop, ⅜ x ⅜

Cork or leather facing

Slides, ⁴⁷⁄₆₄ x ⁶³⁄₆₄ x 17⅜

Housing sides, ¾ x 1

Housing bottom, ⅛ x 3

Drawer kicker, 1⅛ x 1½

3

1

⅛

Slide-stop rabbet, ⅜ x ⅜

Pocket hole

Spacer, ⅝ x 3⅞

Drawer runner, ½ x 1½

can be attached to the primary rail and stretcher or to a secondary rail and stretcher, as was done with the swing leg.

Swing and crane supports

A swing support is a vertical brace, roughly triangular in shape, that pivots between the table's top rail and a lower stretcher to support a leaf. If, instead of a single vertical piece, the support is made of three separate pieces, as shown in the right drawing on p. 93, it is called a crane support.

Like the gate-leg table, swing and crane supports rely on the extra strength of two pivot points for greater strength and stability. The pivot points could be built into the top rail or stretcher, but frequently, they are added to the face. Swing and crane supports are sturdier than apron-mounted swing arms but not as strong as swing legs, which distribute the load directly to the floor. The size of the stretcher will ultimately determine the strength of a swing or crane support.

Slides are less likely to sag

Of all the methods for supporting a drop leaf, my favorite one is the sliding support. It's a neat, clean installation and provides firm support that is less likely to sag than other options.

Sliding supports, as shown in the top photo on p. 94, are relatively easy to make. In just a couple of hours, I can make efficient wooden slides that are a real complement to a drop-leaf table. And if you are not a purist or are pressed for time, you can buy pressed metal hardware that accomplishes nearly the same thing (The Woodworkers' Store, 21801 Industrial Blvd., Rogers Minn. 55374; 800-279-4441).

Hidden supports slide smoothly

My approach is to build a U-shaped channel or housing that holds two sliding supports, one for a leaf on each side of the table, as shown in the bottom photo on the facing page. The design easily could be modified for tables with one leaf. The housing fits between the aprons of the table, and each support slides through a slot cut into the apron. Because this table includes a drawer, the housings also pass through the drawer kickers, which are support rails above the drawer that keep it from drooping when opened.

To create mortises in the kickers in this table, I glued 1-in.-thick stock onto 1/8-in.-thick strips, leaving two 3-in.-wide gaps in each kicker to hold the support housings (see the drawing on p. 95). The glued-up construction let me cut all the parts to size on the tablesaw. And this construction elim-

inated the need for a special process to cut out the mortises. I temporarily clamped the kickers in place at the top of the table's side rails while I fitted the slide housings.

I also made the U-shaped housings by gluing the sides onto 1/8-in.-thick bottoms, leaving enough space between the sides for the slides to bypass each other smoothly. I routed rabbets for the slider stops into each of the side pieces (see the drawing on p. 95). The housing's sides are long enough to span the table's side rails; the housing bottoms are shorter to fit between the kicker bottoms. The housings fit snugly into the gaps left in the kickers.

Tight clearance provides smooth action with no play

The slides have about 1/64-in. clearance for a snug fit inside the housings. The maximum length of the slide is determined by the distance between the side rails, plus the thickness of one side rail, plus 3/8 in. for a finger pull that extends beyond the outside of the rail.

With the supports cut to size, I laid them in position in the housings, with one end extending over the table's side rails, and scribed the intersection on top of the rails with a sharp knife. Then I sawed and chiseled out the slots to allow the supports to extend through the rails. Next I glued stops in the appropriate locations on the sides of each support, and I drilled for and inserted thin, nylon stem bumpers (which are available from The Woodworkers' Store) on both ends of the top of the supports. The bumpers make the supports slide much easier.

Finally, I disassembled and finished all the parts and drilled screw holes though the kickers for attaching the tabletop. Then I glued kickers and support housings into place (see the bottom photo on the facing page), positioned the sliders and attached the tabletops with leaves that were already in place.

DRAWER-DESIGN STRATEGIES

by Gary Rogowski

It's always a wonder to me when I come across an old piece of furniture with drawers that slide as sweetly as they did the day they were made. How is it possible for old drawers to work so well? Odds are they have been weighted down, filled to overflowing, pushed, pulled, slammed home, tipped over and otherwise abused by several generations of owners. Yet if a drawer is well-made, it will fit snugly in its opening and open and close effortlessly, regardless of the season. And it will continue to work that way for a long time.

With so many ways to put a drawer together, which way is best? There's no simple answer, but there are some basic considerations that can help you choose the right corner joint, materials and method of supporting the bottom.

The object is to build a strong, stable, attractive drawer in a reasonable amount of time. How you do this will depend on your skills, tastes and the function of the piece that you are building. I built the drawers shown at left to showcase a number of the best possibilities for drawer construction in a fine case piece. These methods aren't the last word on drawer construction, but they should provide a good starting point.

Function: Make it strong and stable

When I'm working out the design for a piece of furniture that will include a drawer, I think first about function. A file cabinet or tool-box drawer obviously needs to be stronger than a drawer that will hold only socks or a few pencils. And, generally, the deeper a drawer is the stronger it needs to be.

Corner construction

Through dovetail

Pros: Very strong, great mechanical strength and large long-grain to long-grain glue area. The hand-cut through dovetail is aesthetically strong, too. End grain shows on the drawer face, providing a pleasing contrast in some furniture styles.

Cons: The end grain exposed on the face may be inappropriate on more traditionally styled pieces. Comparatively speaking, the dovetail is a time-consuming joint to cut, and it takes practice before you can cut it well. Router jigs used to make through dovetails are relatively expensive, and the resulting joint can look too uniform.

Half-blind dovetail

Pros: As with the through dovetail, half-blind dovetails are very strong and look great, too. And because the joint doesn't show on the drawer face, it's ideal for even the most formal and traditional drawers.

Cons: Even more time-consuming and finnicky to cut by hand than through dovetails. Routed half-blind dovetails look routed because of the minimum width of the pins. Most jigs don't allow flexible spacing of pins and tails.

Rabbeted half dovetail

Pros: Simple to cut (one pass on the router table for each drawer component), simple to clamp and quite handsome. When pinned with dowels, it's a mechanically strong joint.

Cons: Not as strong as through- or half-blind dovetails and without the traditional cachet. All glue-surface area is end grain to long grain, a weaker connection than long grain to long grain.

Sliding dovetail

Pros: Very strong, easy to cut once set up. Can be made so the joint is visible at the top edge of the drawer or so the joint is hidden (stopped).

Cons: Difficult to fit and assemble. The fit should be a bit loose when the joint is dry because glue will start to bind the joint almost immediately. You'll need to work fast once you've applied the glue.

Blind-dado rabbet

Pros: Good production joint. It's quick to cut on the router table once it's set up. With a dedicated bit, setup is quick, too. Joint is hidden from front and looks nice if done well.

Cons: Time-consuming to set up unless you have a dedicated bit, which is expensive. Only fair mechanical strength and all glue-surface area is end grain to long grain. Side edges of drawer front are vulnerable to chipping if they're not beveled slightly.

Drawer joints, like all woodworking joints, derive their strength either from the amount of long-grain glue-surface area shared by the two joined parts or by the way the parts interlock mechanically.

Dovetails make the strongest joints

In a chest of drawers, most any well-made joint will be strong enough because the weight the drawers will have to bear is minimal. But stuff a drawer with reams of paper, a dozen handplanes or a blender, assorted bowls and a Cuisinart, and you've upped the ante.

In situations where I know a drawer is going to have to stand up to some heavy use, I like to use a dovetail joint. Through, half-blind and sliding dovetails (see the photos on p. 98-99) will stand up to almost any use or abuse imaginable. Short of destroying a drawer, you're not likely to see a well-made dovetail joint fail. So choosing one of these three joints becomes a question of aesthetics and efficiency.

A simpler joint in the back

Often a drawer is held together with two kinds of joints: something a little fancier in the front where it will show and something simpler in the back where strength, not appearance, is the primary consideration. In the chest shown at left, I joined the backs of the top four drawers to the sides with sliding dovetails because they're strong, and I can make them quickly with a router.

There's one situation in which you can't use a sliding dovetail at the back of a drawer: when you want to capture a plywood drawer bottom on all four sides, as I did on the bottom drawer in this chest. For that drawer, I used dado-rabbet joints at the back corners. The dadoes run from top to bottom on the drawer sides, just in from the ends. The back is rabbeted to engage the dado and is flush with the back end of the sides.

Quartersawn lumber is best

Another functional consideration is stability: how much the drawer will move with seasonal changes in humidity. A drawer that's swollen shut is obviously useless, but one with a huge gap at the top isn't very attractive. So I try to use quartersawn lumber for the sides and backs of drawers whenever possible. It's much more dimensionally stable than flatsawn stock and less likely to warp or twist.

Regardless of whether I'm using quartersawn or flatsawn lumber, I make sure the drawer stock is thoroughly seasoned. I also try to let it acclimate in my shop for a few weeks before working it.

Choosing wood for sides, back, runners

For drawer sides and backs, I generally select a wood that's different from the fronts. Secondary wood saves a little money. And there's no need to waste really spectacular lumber on drawer sides or backs. I use a wood that moves about the same amount seasonally as the drawer fronts and is long-wearing. I also use this secondary wood for the drawer runners. This prevents the sides from wearing a groove in the runners or the runners from wearing down the sides.

Using a secondary wood for the sides of a drawer also can set up an interesting contrast when the drawer is opened, especially with a lighter-colored wood.

Aim for a thin drawer side

Drawer-side thickness is a concern for both structural and aesthetic reasons. What you're trying to achieve is a drawer that's light, strong and well-proportioned. For this chest, I used $3/8$-in.-thick drawer sides for the top pair of drawers. I added $1/16$ in. thickness to the sides and back of each descending drawer. Graduated drawers distinguish this piece from production work; each drawer has sufficient strength and pleasing proportions.

Aesthetics: Make it attractive and appropriate

The next consideration is appearance. A nailed rabbet joint, for example, may work perfectly well but just wouldn't make it in a reproduction American highboy. All of the joints I used in this chest of drawers are attractive, but some are more refined than others. So the choice of joinery, especially at the front of the drawer, may hinge on the expectations or tastes of the client and the style of the piece.

To my eye, the through dovetail, the half-blind dovetail and the rabbeted half dovetail work better aesthetically with this piece than do the sliding dovetail or blind-dado rabbet. But for drawers in a kitchen island or a child's bureau, I'd probably go with the sliding dovetail or the blind-dado rabbet because neither of these furniture pieces requires fancy joinery.

Efficiency: Can I make it quickly and easily?

Ease and speed of construction are related concerns, especially if you make your living as a furnituremaker. As a professional, I have to weigh the time it takes to cut and assemble a joint against what it adds to the piece. I also have to know whether the client is willing to pay for the extra labor. If you're an amateur woodworker, time probably is less of a concern, but there will still be projects you just want to finish.

The relative difficulty of making a particular joint also may be a consideration. If you've never cut dovetails by hand before, it's probably a good idea to practice before you start cutting into those figured-maple drawer fronts.

If you have no desire to cut dovetails by hand, a number of router jigs will cut dovetails that are just as strong or stronger than hand-cut ones. But with a few exceptions,

they all give you dovetails that look rigidly uniform and machine-made. These may not be the right choice on a piece of furniture that traditionally would have had hand-cut dovetails. And even if routed dovetails work for you aesthetically, there's a learning curve for most of these jigs. So while there may be some gain in efficiency over time, you shouldn't plan to buy a jig on Saturday to speed you through your dovetails on Sunday.

A router can help you make other good-looking, simple joints that are plenty strong. The sliding dovetail and the blind-dado rabbet on the bottom two drawers of this chest fit the bill on all counts.

Supporting drawer bottoms

Corner joinery is only one facet of drawer construction. There's also the question of how to support the drawer bottom. What's wrong with a simple groove cut near the bottom of the drawer sides? Not a thing for most work (see the top drawing on p. 102), but if you check out a really first-rate antique, chances are good that the drawer will be riding on slips (see the top left drawing on p. 103).

Drawer slips are strips of wood glued to the bottom inside faces of the drawer sides. They sit flush with the bottom of the side and are grooved to accept a drawer bottom. Designed to increase the running surface of the drawer, slips prevent the drawer side from wearing a groove in the runner. They also prevent a thin drawer side from being weakened by a groove. I used drawer slips on two of the drawers on p. 102: one with a plywood bottom and one with a rabbeted, solid-cedar bottom.

Slips are more than just functional additions to a drawer. They add a measure of finish and formality that catches your eye. I didn't add any decorative elements to the slips in this drawer, but you could bead the top inside edge of the slip, cove it or round

Bottom construction

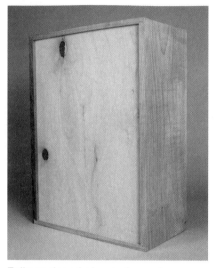

Fully enclosed plywood panel

Solid raised panel in a groove

Plywood panel in a drawer slip

Rabbeted solid panel in a drawer slip

Mix and match: You can support a drawer bottom in grooves cut in the drawer sides or in slips glued to the sides. Drawer bottoms can be made of plywood or solid wood. Either material is compatible with either method of support. Your choice will be based on time, cost and the piece's function.

Grooves

Grooved drawer sides provide plenty of support for most drawer bottoms, as long as the drawers aren't going to carry a lot of weight. Sides should be sized proportionally to the width of the drawer.

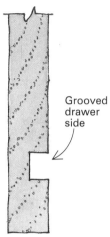

Grooved drawer side

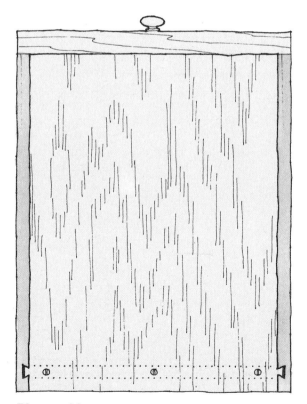

Plywood bottom can be supported on three sides and screwed to the back of the drawer (above) or totally enclosed and supported in grooves on all four sides (top photo at left).

Slips

Drawer slips add strength and rigidity and increase the drawer's bearing surface on the runners. Slips can be simple, grooved pieces of wood, or they can be made more decorative, as shown at right.

Slip profiles

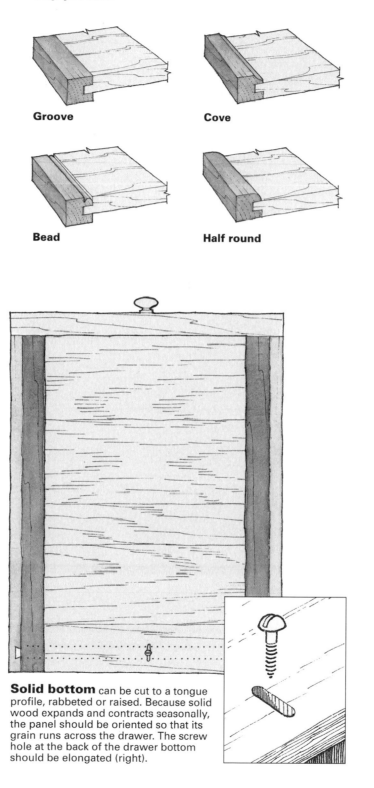

Groove

Cove

Bead

Half round

Drawer side

Slip

Solid-bottom profiles

Tongue

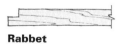

Rabbet

Raised panel

Solid bottom can be cut to a tongue profile, rabbeted or raised. Because solid wood expands and contracts seasonally, the panel should be oriented so that its grain runs across the drawer. The screw hole at the back of the drawer bottom should be elongated (right).

it over to add more visual interest, as shown in the drawings on p. 102.

Plywood or solid wood?

The other big decision is whether to make the drawer bottoms from plywood or from solid wood.

Plywood is stronger but not traditional

Plywood has many advantages over solid wood, but for some purists, it is simply unacceptable.

Plywood is dimensionally stable, so you don't have to take wood movement into consideration. It is stronger for a given thickness than solid material, so you can use a thinner piece: $1/4$-in. plywood is thick enough for a drawer bottom (I normally use a $1/2$-in. panel if it's solid wood). This also makes plywood a good choice if you're concerned with weight.

One problem with using plywood is that the actual thickness of a $1/4$-in. sheet is about $7/32$ in. That means that if you rout a $1/4$-in. groove in a slip or in your drawer sides, the plywood panel will flop around. Instead, I use a $3/16$-in. bit and make two passes. I get a perfect fit, but it takes more time. Of course, there are dado sets available that will plow a $7/32$-in. groove, but you can't always run the groove the length of the drawer piece. On some drawer fronts, for instance, you need a stopped groove.

Installing solid-wood bottoms

For solid-wood drawer bottoms, the grain must run side to side in the drawer, rather than front to back, so wood expansion won't push the drawer apart and shrinkage won't create a gap at the sides. I usually either rabbet or raise a panel on a solid-wood drawer bottom so the edge is thinner than the rest of the field (see the solid-bottom profiles on p. 103). This lets me plow a smaller groove in the drawer sides. The result is a strong, sturdy panel that will not weaken the drawer slips or sides excessively.

A rabbeted panel can be slid in with the raised portion facing either up or down. When I use drawer slips and a rabbeted panel, I put the panel in with the raised portion up, mark the panel, remove it and then plane, scrape and sand the panel so it's flush with the drawer slips. With the more traditional raised panel, I position the panel bevel-side down.

Keeping the drawer bottom in place

I don't glue drawer bottoms in place. It's easier to repair a drawer if the bottom just slides right out. To keep solid-wood drawer bottoms from sagging, I screw them to the drawer back with a single pan-head screw and elongate the hole so the bottom can move (see the drawing detail on p. 103).

In spite of its strength, a $1/4$-in. plywood panel is quite flexible, so I usually drive two or three screws into the drawer back. Otherwise, the bottom will sag (see the bottom drawing on p. 102).

Another possibility for plywood is to enclose it on all four sides (see the top photo on p. 102). Because plywood is dimensionally stable, there's no need to leave the back open.

METAL DRAWER-SLIDE OPTIONS

by Jim Tolpin

Let's face it. Metal drawer slides aren't pretty. You wouldn't install them on a Queen Anne dressing table or an Arts-and-Crafts style chest of drawers. But if you're making built-ins where the drawers will get lots and lots of use, whether in the kitchen, the office or even in your own woodshop, "pretty" may have to step aside for "practical."

Metal drawer slides aren't about to replace traditional wooden drawer parts in American period furniture reproductions. Some furnituremakers are never going to warm up to the idea, and some buyers of well-crafted furniture just won't accept them. But drawer hardware does have some real advantages.

Beauty and the beast—High-end cabinetry and steel drawer slides make an enduring marriage in kitchens, offices and even workshops. Because drawer slides can operate smoothly under very heavy loads (up to 175 lbs.) and because they keep drawers from sticking, they're perfect in heavy-use situations.

European-style slides mean smaller drawers both in width and depth. The drawer boxes must be 1 in. narrower and almost 1 in. shallower.

Bottom-mount (Euro-style) slides____

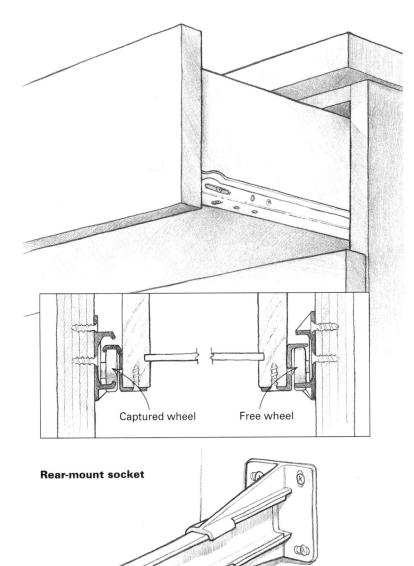

Captured wheel   Free wheel

Rear-mount socket

Metal slides let you pull out a heavily laden drawer with a fingertip, and they let you shut the drawer with a casual push. You never have to worry about drawers sticking or binding. And you don't have to worry about the wood-to-wood wear and tear that inevitably happens over years of use.

If you're not familiar with all the different kinds of slides on the market, not to mention all the makes and models, finding your way through the array of available hardware can be tough and frustrating. Do you want the full-extension, heavy-duty, all-ball-bearing Accuride slides for $32 a pair? Or will the Blum single-extension, double-roller, epoxy-coated slides for $5.75 a pair do just fine? Do you want side-mount slides or bottom mount? And what's the difference between the self-closing feature and the stay-shut feature that many slides have?

Drawer slides come in four basic types

From a cabinetmaker's point of view, the most logical way to categorize drawer-slide hardware is not by cost, feature or appearance but by where the hardware mounts on the drawer. That's where hardware has the most affect on design and construction of cabinetry. Certain types of hardware are suitable for particular designs and construction methods; other types are not.

With mounting location in mind, there are four major types of drawer-slide hardware: Bottom-mount (European-style) slides, which attach to the bottom edges of the drawer sides; side-mount slides, which attach directly to the sides of the drawer; under-mount slides, which attach to the drawer bottom, one on each side; and center mount (the only single-slide system I'll describe here), which fastens to the center of the drawer bottom. Within each of these categories, there's a good deal of variation on the basic concept, and there are a number of different slides to choose from in each. Most manufacturers make most types of slides, so I'll mention brand names only when it seems appropriate.

In addition to the four types shown here, there are several other kinds of drawer hardware available, such as systems that use wheels without slides or slides without wheels. These designs really don't qualify as true slide systems nor do they, to my mind, perform as well and last as long as real slide systems do. So I haven't included any of them.

Please keep in mind that terminology can be a problem when studying up on drawer slides because catalogers and manufacturers sometimes call the same thing by different names, especially when referring to mounting locations. But the definitions above jibe with most of the product literature I've come across.

Bottom-mount (European-style) slides

These slides mount along the bottom edges of the drawer sides and to the inside walls of the cabinet. Their steel runners are epoxy coated in white, almond or black for the sake of appearance and to prevent rust, which protects and extends the life of the nylon rollers. Most Euro slides are single-extension, and they open the drawer to three-fourths its length. But some bottom

mounts are dual-slide and full-extension. All bottom-mount slides are either self-closing or have a stay-shut feature. The self-closing action of some bottom mounts is a major benefit, and you may need it badly enough to use these slides in places where they're not particularly well-suited.

The primary advantage of bottom-mount slides is their good performance and low cost. Though visible at the sides of the drawers, they are not as obtrusive as side-mount hardware. (If, for example, you choose white melamine for the drawer boxes, the white coated slides will blend right in).

Another advantage is that these slides are easy to install. Especially if you are working with Euro-style frameless cabinets and using a 32mm grid system and system screws. (European cabinet construction employs a modular 32mm grid for the efficient use of sheet goods and standardized, adjustable hardware.) One more big plus: the side-to-side fit of the drawer in the opening is not critical. In fact, you have a full $\frac{1}{8}$ in. of drawer width to play with. This is because one side uses a captive wheel-in-rail, and the other side uses an open track that gives the wheel some room to roam, as the drawing on the facing page shows.

Now for the disadvantages of Euro-style slides. First, you have to make the drawer box at least 1 in. narrower than the drawer opening. You also have to make the box about 1 in. shallower than the opening because when you insert the drawer into its tracks, you have to get the slide wheels up and over the wheels on the fixed runner. Second, you can't use most varieties of Euro-style bottom mounts if you intend to fully recess the drawer front inside the cabinet because the stay-shut action of the slide drops the drawer box about $\frac{3}{16}$ in. when it's closed. The result—you get a big, sloppy-looking gap at the top of the drawer.

Installation tips

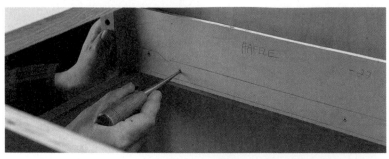

Jig aids in aligning drawer slides—Make up a simple jig with drawer-slide hardware traced on it. This will ensure the slide is properly aligned.

Shim slides to adjust the fit— Use pieces of sandpaper to shim drawer slides to obtain the correct opening width. All runners and guides should be installed so that they are level with one another and square to the face of the cabinet.

Side-mount slides

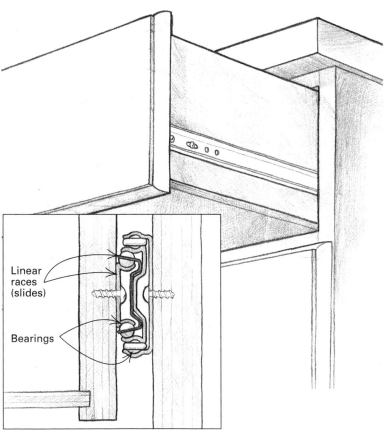

Linear races (slides)

Bearings

Best uses
Euro-style slides can be used successfully in face-frame cabinetry. But I recommend using them for moderate-duty, full-overlay drawers in frameless cabinets for kitchens and baths and in other cabinets where drawer fronts and doors overlay the case and don't have to fit inside frames with tight tolerances. Their low-profile appearance, ease of installation, good performance and low cost make bottom mounts well-suited to economy-minded makers of frameless, Euro-style cabinetry.

Installation tips
In frameless cabinets, installation is straightforward and unremarkable. But not so on face-frame cabinets. When I just have to use Euro slides in face-frame cabinets (let's say my clients demand self-closing drawers), I design the case sides to be flush to the inside edge of the face frames wherever possible. This lets me mount the hardware directly to the inside of the case (just as I would on a frameless cabinet) in predrilled system holes. If I can't make the face frame and case sides flush, I block out the case sides with scraps of plywood and mount the fixed part of the slide right on the blocking.

There's one other way around this problem, and it's not a good one. Most manufacturers of Euro slides offer what's usually called a rear-mount socket (see the drawing detail on p. 106), which lets you attach the fixed slide to the rear of the case. I use these things only as a last resort because they are difficult to install and adjust. And once properly installed and adjusted, the flimsy plastic that most of these sockets are made of sometimes cracks if the screws are over-tightened.

Side-mount slides
These telescoping slides are made of a fixed channel and two steel runners, which all mesh with one another through races of nylon or steel ball bearings (see the drawing at left). Mounted to the sides of the drawer boxes, these slides offer smooth, quiet, wobble-free motion. They all extend fully, and most will support a lot of weight and still operate with minimal effort. Most side

Drawer-slide terminology

Full extension: Multiple, telescoping slides let you pull the drawer clear of the cabinet, giving full access.

Single extension: A single slide lets you pull the drawer about three-quarters open. You have to reach inside the cabinet to get to things in the back of the drawer.

Self closing: A design that closes drawers automatically when they get within 2 to 4 in. from the face of the cabinet. This keeps you from snagging your shins or banging your hips on partially open drawers.

Stay shut: A depression, or detent, in the slide or in the fixed track holds a pair of rollers to keep the drawer from drifting open, like parking your car with its front wheels in a pair of pot holes. Some slides use friction catches to stay shut. Beware the pot-hole slides if you're installing inset drawer fronts that must fit closely all around.

Load ratings: Whether touted as heavy duty or not, most cabinet-drawer slides—single extension and full extension, are rated at a carrying capacity of 75 lbs. to 100 lbs., which is about right for most conventional installations. Some light-duty slides are rated at 50 lbs. to 60 lbs. Really heavy-duty slides meant for filing cabinet drawers are rated at 150 lbs. to 175 lbs.

Rollers vs. ball bearings: As a general rule, single-extension slides use plastic or nylon wheels or rollers, and most full-extension slides use ball bearings, sometimes steel, sometimes plastic, sometimes a combination of both, in linear races between the telescoping slides.

Epoxy finish: Available on single-extension, European-style slides, an epoxy coating over the steel makes the hardware easy to clean as well as chip and rust resistant. Also, the slick finish makes for less wear on the rollers and smoother action.

---

mounts are made of zinc-plated steel, but some varieties now come with black or white epoxy coatings for a less in-your-face industrial look.

Reliable performance and durability are the chief advantages of side-mount slides. But on the downside, they are intrusively visible (a nice way of saying they're just plain ugly), they don't have a self-closing feature—a major drawback in high-traffic areas—and they aren't all that easy to install correctly.

Best uses

Superior performance makes side mounts the hardware of choice for any drawer that must carry heavy loads and needs to be extended fully. I recommend them highly for use in either Euro-style frameless cabinets or in furniture-grade, face-frame cabinetry where the drawer fronts have to be fully recessed into the case. Because there is no drop action when the drawer closes, as is

Center-mount slides

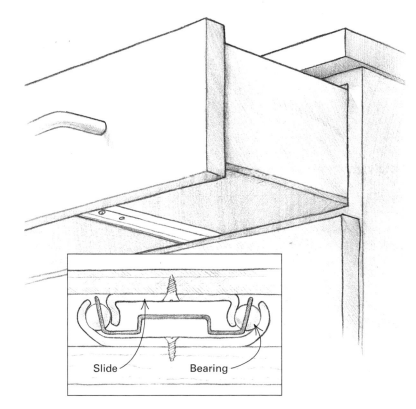

Slide

Bearing

the case with most Euro-style slides, you can achieve close, even margins around all four sides of the front. Ugly aside, I use these slides in really good pieces of furniture, such as desks, filing cabinets and entertainment centers, where the drawers have to be opened often and must support heavy loads.

Installation tips

These slides must be installed to very close tolerances, or they just won't work the way that they're supposed to. So to ensure a precise installation, I begin by laying out their positions on the case sides, marking the exact location of the drawers and their hardware. I mount the slides to the centerline of the drawer-box sides and the fixed channels to the corresponding position of these centerlines on the inside of the cabinet. I'm also careful when sizing the boxes to the openings, making them a precise 1 in. narrower.

When I mount the hardware, I get all the parts in approximate position using a pair of screws through the elongated mounting holes—the vertical holes on the drawer-box slides and the horizontal holes on the fixed channel or runner. When I've made the necessary adjustments, I lock the hardware in place with additional screws through the non-elongated holes.

Center-mount slides

Designed to be used singly, one of these slides mounts under the drawer box at the centerline, so it is largely hidden from view. But it won't handle much weight (less than 50 lbs.). Some center-mount slides are not suitable for high-quality cabinetry or furniture work because they make for wobbly drawers and because they are noisy and rough in operation.

As far as I know, there are only two makes of center-mount slides worth putting in decent cabinetwork. They are the

Comparing drawer-slide hardware

	Type of slide	Weight capacity (static lbs.)	Extension range	Self closing available	Visibility on extension
	Bottom mount (European style)	50 lbs. to 100 lbs.	Three-quarter or full	Yes	Guide visible on outside lower edges
	Side mount	75 lbs. to 175 lbs.	Full extension and over-travel (1½ in. greater than full)	No	Guide prominently visible on side of box
	Center mount	35 lbs. to 50 lbs.	Three-quarter	No	Hidden
	Under mount	75 lbs. to 100 lbs.	Three-quarter or full	Yes	Hidden

Accuride Series 1029 and the Knape and Vogt (KV) Series 1500. Both have smooth, wobble-free action thanks to their meshed steel runners and ball-bearing races. For drawers wider than 12 in., I would install two slides to ensure smooth, stable operation and to handle the extra weight that bigger drawers always wind up carrying.

But even the best center-mount slides have several disadvantages. They are the lightest duty of the slide hardware systems, and they are not available in either self-closing or full-extension versions. Both the KV and Accuride models are three-quarter extension, exposing $16\frac{1}{2}$ in. of a $22\frac{1}{2}$-in. drawer.

Best uses

I would use these slides primarily in face-frame cabinets (the front of the fixed channel must attach to a drawer divider) that include small, light-duty drawers in which I need to maximize drawer capacity. Center-mount slides are the only ones that allow you to make drawers that are fully as wide as the drawer openings. All the other hardware systems require from $\frac{3}{16}$ in. to $\frac{1}{2}$ in. of clearance on each side. Because center mounts are visible only on the underside of the box, they're good choices for people who just can't bear the sight of metal contraptions defiling their well-crafted drawers.

Installation tips

For center-mount slides to work properly, you must install them level and precisely square to the face of the cabinet. If you use a pair, they have to be installed parallel to prevent binding or resistance. Because the slides mount to the drawer bottom, the fixed runner can't be mounted to the case side. It's attached instead to the drawer divider in front and to the rear wall of the cabinet in back. And this means using one of those rear-mount sockets. But the center-mount sockets, because they're made of stamped

Finish	Ease of installation and adjustment	Cost	Applications	Clearances between drawer box and opening (check manufacturer's exact specifications)
Epoxy coating in white and almond	Easy	$7 to $15 a pair	Kitchen and other built-in cabinets	Each side: ½ in. Top: ¾ in. Bottom: ⅛ in.
Steel, black and white coatings available	Moderate difficulty	$15 to $35 a pair	For all styles of cabinetry, but necessary in cabinets requiring high weight capacity and full extension	Each side: ½ in. Top: Not critical Bottom: Not critical
Zinc-plated or coated brown/buff	Easy	$6 each	Light-duty utility case work	Each side: Not critical Top: Not critical Bottom: ½ in. for Accuride, ¹³⁄₁₆ in. for Knapeand Vogt (KV); others vary by manufacturer
Steel	Precision in building and sizing drawer required	$20 to $25 a pair	High-end cabinet work and furniture	Each side: ¹³⁄₁₆ in. Top: ⅛ in. Bottom: ⅜ in.

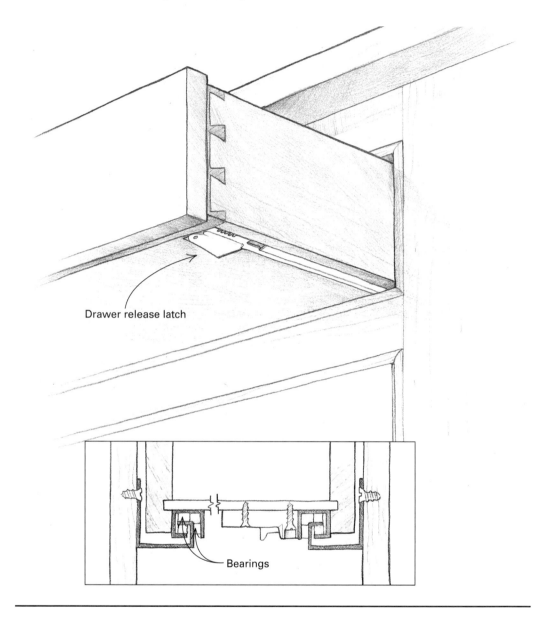

Drawer release latch

Bearings

steel, aren't quite as cheesy as the ones that come with some makes of Euro slides.

These rear sockets can be difficult to position correctly, though. I use a T-square rig with a torpedo level taped to it to find the mounting position at the rear of the case. I reference the square off the drawer divider and watch the bubble. I use pan-head screws for more holding power.

Under-mount (hidden) slides

I've saved the best for last. I've just recently discovered under-mount slides, and they seem, from my brief experience with them, to have it all: The smoothest action of any slide system, positive self-closing, heavy-duty construction (rated for 75 lb. loads or greater), latch-in drawer connect and dis-connect, three-quarter or full extension, and minimal clearances between drawer and case

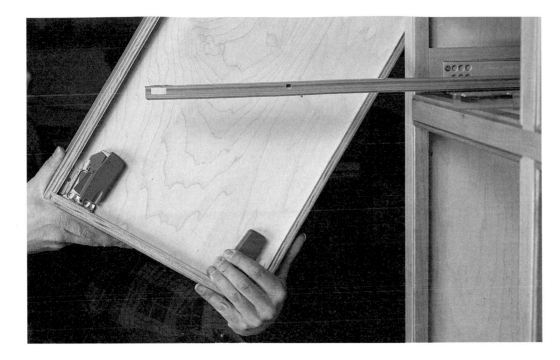

Fit for fine furniture— Completely concealed, under-mount drawer slides combine premium quality, high performance and design freedom.

sides. But best of all, they're hidden, which is a good thing because naked to the light of day, they're the ugliest drawer slides you've ever seen.

These precision-made fittings, which mount to the bottom against the sides of the drawers, feature a steel slide that moves in and out on two sets of ball or roller bearings instead of just one. One set of bearings provides vertical support, the other gives lateral support. The result is a firm, wobble-free, silky-smooth action that other slides don't have.

So surely, there must be something wrong with these things. I have tried to find it, but I can voice only three minor quibbles. Under mounts are on the expensive side. Only one brand offers a full-extension model, and these slides are the most demanding of all to install.

I've been able to locate five manufacturers of under-mount slides: Blum "Tandem," Fulterer "2130" series, the Mepla "Dynamic FFD 831," Hettich "Quadro" and Häfele "Soft Roller 40." There may be others out there, but I haven't found them.

Best uses

For high-end work. Especially in fine cabinetry and furniture with fully recessed drawer fronts and doors. And, yes, despite what I said at the start, I'd use these slides in that Arts-and-Crafts style chest of drawers.

Installation tips

When installing under-mount slides to the bottom of the drawer box, be sure to use the drilling jig supplied by the manufacturer. This will ensure that the quick-release mounting plates are properly oriented to the drawer box. Drawer-box dimensioning is critical here. And this includes the thickness of the drawer sides, as well as the width and depth of the box. So I'm especially careful to make the drawer according to the directions specified by the manufacturer. Note that the inset of the drawer-bottom panel (usually about 1/2 in.) is also a critical dimension for this type of slide. You can adjust the drawer box up and down by turning a fitting on the drawer-box mounting plate.

FIVE

Construction Options for Cabinets

Basic box or carcase construction underlies a lot of different furniture. Boxes, chests, drawers, chests of drawers, kitchen cabinets, many types of built-ins, and desks all are essentially variations on the idea of a box. You might even say that a table is really a box with a couple of sides missing, but that's pushing the point. In short, box construction techniques are among the most useful because of their almost universal application. The dovetail, for instance, is a traditional box joint. But consider how many other applications that joint has, from the sliding dovetail to drawer dividers.

This chapter describes a wide range of options for box and carcase-related construction, making it the largest in the book. The result is a rich offering of options for many of the most common tasks in building furniture. For example, Gary Rogowski brings together the best options for assembling drawers and building boxes. He compares and contrasts all the common joints, from rabbets to dovetails. Graham Blackburn explores the options for building frame-and-panel doors. Chris Becksvoort discusses strategies for designing the back sides of carcases to be attractive rather than afterthoughts.

There are also sections on options for traditional cabinet face frames, for large-cabinet knockdown joinery, for supporting cabinet shelves, and for closing cabinet doors with latches, catches, and locks.

Reading these sections for their particular applications is useful in itself, but there's more. If you read between the lines you'll find more than one application for most techniques. For example, face-frame construction is essentially frame-without-panel construction, and all the ideas can be exchanged (within reason). Knockdown joinery, though most useful for large cabinets, could also be applied to smaller pieces for reasons other than portability. This chapter will show you many options. It's up to you how you use them.

A DOZEN WAYS TO BUILD A BOX

by Gary Rogowski

Twenty years of furnituremaking experience separate the author's nailed, butt-joined carpenter's toolbox from his pegged, finger-joined walnut jewelry box. Drawer fronts are joined to drawer sides with pinned, half-blind, half dovetails.

The first box I ever built I put together with enough nails to build a small house. "Can't be too strong," was my motto. That toolbox is still together, too. But in building furniture for the last 20 years, I have learned a few more ways of putting boxes together, from plain and simple to elaborate and complex—all without those nails (see the photos on the facing page and at right).

Box construction is a basic building block of furnituremaking. Whether you want to build a desk or a kitchen cabinet, an entertainment center or a jewelry box, knowing how to build a box that is both functional and stylistically appropriate is crucial. The more joinery options you're familiar (and comfortable) with, the greater your furnituremaking vocabulary and the greater the chances that you will consider your furniture projects successful.

There are three essential considerations when deciding on the joinery for a box: function, economy and style. Ask yourself what the box is for. A box's function will usually help determine appropriate types of joinery for the project based on how much work is involved (economy) and on the look you're trying to achieve (style). A carpenter's toolbox or a birdhouse doesn't really require anything more sophisticated than butt joints. Kitchen cabinets, because you generally need quite a few of them, are well-suited to simple joinery techniques, but they also must be strong. There's no point in dovetailing these cabinets; it would take forever and not serve any but a decorative purpose. A splined or biscuit-joined miter, however, is a very good compromise.

Other boxes, whether they house your fine silver or your prized handplane collection, may justify the time and effort required to dovetail a carcase precisely. The attention you pay to detail and the emphasis placed on the joinery as a design feature, are in keeping with the valued contents of those boxes.

There are many ways to put together a box. I discuss a dozen here, but there are at

least another dozen besides. The methods I've presented here, though, collectively form a good initial "vocabulary" of woodworking joinery. I've also provided some basic guidelines on choosing and cutting joinery, both for solid wood and for plywood and other sheet goods. No magazine article can cover such a vast topic in depth, however, so I've also listed a few books on joinery that treat the subject in much greater depth.

Knowing your alternatives just gets you started. Choosing the right joint for the job and acquiring the requisite skills is still up to you. Fortunately, as with most aspects of woodworking, there will be no one right answer (see the photo on p. 123), and every foray into unfamiliar territory will add to your repertoire.

Butt joints

Butt joints are the simplest and quickest way of putting a box together. Boards are simply cut to length at 90° both to the board's edge and to its face (a square cut) and then glued at the ends and fastened with nails or screws (see figure 1).

The problem with butt joints in solid stock is that you're joining long grain to end grain. That is an inherently weak connection because glue doesn't bind well to the open-ended wood fibers of the end grain. A box that's joined with butt joints won't last

forever, especially if it's subject to a lot of abuse, but for applications such as garden frames or birdhouses, it's fine. Often, too, these kinds of utilitarian projects are made of plywood, which provides a better glue surface than solid stock for this joint.

Rabbet joints

The advantage of a simple rabbet joint over a butt joint is that the glue surface area is larger. It's still a long-grain to end-grain joint, but the greater surface area helps somewhat. Another advantage of the rabbet joint is that by cutting the rabbet at the end of one board to precisely the thickness of the mating board, your boards are automatically flush (see figure 2). Window frames are often made this way.

Rabbets can be planed by hand, cut on the tablesaw or routed. If the box is small and will not be put under a lot of stress, the glue joint should hold up fine by itself without mechanical fasteners. For larger pieces, however, and where greater strength will obviously be necessary, it's a good idea to nail or screw the joint, or pin it with dowels. Even with plywood, which is

often joined with rabbet joints to make cabinets, the addition of fasteners is probably a good idea, providing a measure of insurance.

A double rabbet joint has a still greater glue surface area and, when cut on the tablesaw or routed on a router table, is easily set up. By setting bit or blade height and depth precisely the same, the boards will mate perfectly (see figure 3).

Another variation on the rabbet joint is the dado rabbet. This joint's greatest asset, besides its being relatively easy to create, is that it possesses some mechanical strength by virtue of its captured dado (see figure 4). This joint is best used with plywood, however, because in solid stock, the end of the board extending past the dado is susceptible to breaking, especially when you're fit-

ting the joint. The grain is just so short there that a little too much pressure can cause the end to pop right off. Still, if fitted carefully, using a thin dado and keeping it as far from the corner as possible, the joint can be assembled without a great deal of trepidation.

If you want the ends of the dadoed boards to be flush with the sides of the mating boards, it's crucial that you lay out the joint accurately. That's because the placement of the dado locates the rabbeted box side. If the dado is not set in far enough from the corner, the rabbeted side will remain proud of the corner; if the dado is set in too far, you have some short end grain to remove after glue-up.

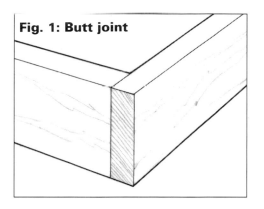

Fig. 1: Butt joint

Figure 1: The butt joint is the simplest of woodworking joints, but in solid stock, it is also the weakest because of the long-grain to end-grain glue surface.

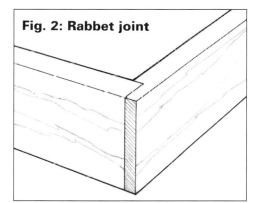

Fig. 2: Rabbet joint

Figure 2: A rabbet joint has a greater glue surface area than a butt joint and, therefore, is stronger. Additionally, with an accurately cut rabbet, the mating board will automatically set flush to the end of the rabbeted board.

Figure 3: The double rabbet joint has an even greater glue surface area than a rabbet joint and is easy to set up on the tablesaw or router table.

Figure 4: The dado rabbet joint possesses mechanical strength in one direction because of the captured dado.

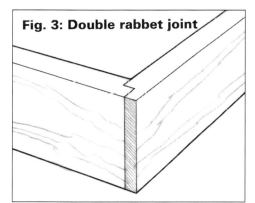

Fig. 3: Double rabbet joint

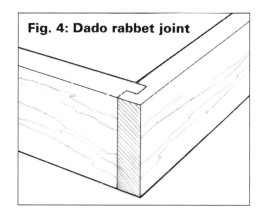

Fig. 4: Dado rabbet joint

Miter joints

Both butt and rabbet joints show end grain from one side of the corner. To avoid this or to carry a decorative edge around a box, mitered corners can be used (see figure 5). Depending on their size, miters can be cut on a miter saw, a sliding compound-miter saw or on a tablesaw.

On the tablesaw, I set the blade at 45° (for a four-sided box) and cut the miters with the box sides lying flat in a standard sliding crosscut jig. To ensure that the resulting joint is really 90°, I cut mating ends of a joint on opposing faces of the blade. This way, if the blade is a half of a degree over or under 45°, it's made up for with the cut on the second board.

Because miter cuts land somewhere between end grain and long grain, strengthening them makes sense. There are many ways of doing this, but two of the strongest and most attractive ways are the use of splines and of keys (see figures 6 and 7).

For a splined miter, a groove needs to be cut before gluing up the joint. To do this, I flip the box sides over in the crosscut jig so that the miter is facing down. The blade is still set at 45°, which is 90° to the miter. I locate the groove as far toward the inside corner of the miter as I safely can (thus

allowing for a wider spline) and clamp a stop block in place so that both pieces will be grooved in the same spot. Then I just pass the box sides over the blade (see the photo at right).

I cut splines either from plywood or solid stock. I use plywood splines for smaller or plywood boxes only because the plywood will not move with changes in humidity. When using solid splines, I always orient the grain in the same direction as the grain of the box sides. This way, the spline moves with the box. It's also a stronger construction. Even though a spline is fragile before it's installed (because it's a length of perpendicularly oriented, short-grained wood), once it's in the carcase, the spline's grain bridges the miter. I always test-fit the splines before gluing, checking especially to see that they aren't too deep for the grooves.

Another way of strengthening a miter joint is to glue in splines or keys across the joint after the miter has been glued together (see figure 7). The grooves for these joints can be cut on the tablesaw with a router or by hand.

For smaller boxes, I use a simple jig that clamps to my tablesaw's crosscut jig and that holds the box sides up at 45° to the

Cutting the groove for a spline in a miter joint is simple using a clamped stop block in a sliding crosscut jig. The stop block ensures that the groove for the spline is positioned in the same place in both boards being glued together.

table (see the top photo on the facing page). I set blade height at about two-thirds the thickness of the joint, so I only have to clean up the keys on the outside of the box. Then, either holding the box firmly in the jig or clamping it in, I pass the entire setup over the blade. Because I only use this setup for relatively narrow boxes (drawers and such), I cut three key grooves, which make positioning of the jig straightforward: one groove equidistant from either edge of the board and one in the center.

Larger boxes require more support for a safe cut, and even though larger jigs can be made for the tablesaw, it's safer and much more accurate to keep the workpiece still and move the tool—in this case, a router—over the workpiece.

I made the fixture in the photo at left above so that I could rout grooves

in a chest of drawers with mitered corners. The jig is centered on the corner of the carcase, at 45° to it, and is supported by angled blocks underneath it. The whole fixture is clamped together and to the carcase. The slots in the face of the jig are sized to fit my plunge router that's outfitted with a template guide. Using a straight bit, I rout grooves across the corners.

I plane the keys, so they're just proud of the corner of the box and then glue them into place, long grain across the corner. Once the glue has set, I cut the key nearly flush with the carcase and plane and sand the keys perfectly flush. By using a contrasting wood, this joint can be made attractive as well as strong (see the bottom photo on the facing page).

The author's jig for cutting grooves for keys clamps right into his crosscut box. For boxes that fit safely into this jig, three keys provide plenty of strength.

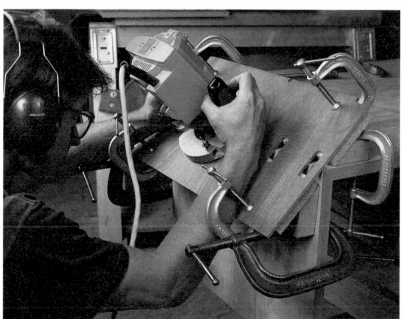

Keyed miters—Two sides of an alder toy box (left) show how attractive a keyed miter joint can be. To rout key grooves in big mitered carcases (above), it's safer with a simple jig.

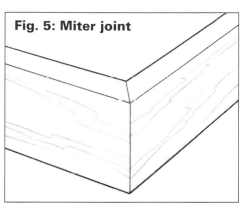

Fig. 5: Miter joint

Figure 5: Mitered joints look more "finished" generally than corners with exposed end grain, but miters are also trickier to cut precisely, which is critical if the joint is to close up nicely.

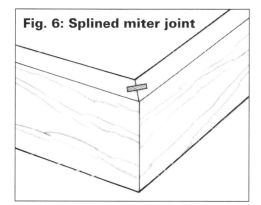

Fig. 6: Splined miter joint

Figure 6: A splined miter joint is considerably stronger than a simple miter joint. Whether plywood or solid wood is used for the spline, long grain bridges the miter and a long-grain to long-grain glue surface area results.

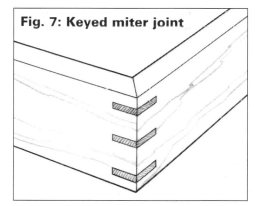

Fig. 7: Keyed miter joint

Figure 7: Keyed miter joints, like splined miters, are stronger than simple miter joints because of the long-grain to long-grain glue surface. The keyed miter joint is glued up as a simple miter joint, and then grooves for the keys are either cut or routed. The keys are cut oversized and then trimmed flush after they've been installed and the glue has set up.

Solid-wood corners for sheet goods

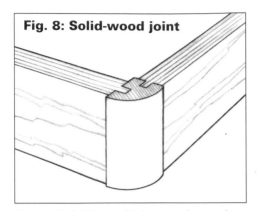

Fig. 8: Solid-wood joint

Figure 8: Solid-wood joints can be used with panels of plywood or some other sheet stock to create strong, attractive boxes of almost any size. The corner block can be oversized and rounded over (as it is here) or shaped in some other way. Or it can be the same thickness as the carcase sides so that it's less noticeable.

When building a carcase of plywood or some other sheet stock, it's possible to use a solid-wood corner and a tongue-and-groove joint. Grooves are generally cut into the solid corners with a tablesaw or router, and then the corresponding tongues are cut into the plywood or particleboard sides. It's also possible to tenon the sheet stock into the solid corners at full thickness. The joint is glued over the full length of the corner piece, which is oriented with its grain running along its length (see figure 8).

This joint is not suitable for solid stock because the corner must be oriented lengthwise to be strong. What you'd end up with if you glued in solid panels for the full length of the corner would be a cross-grain construction resulting in either a failed joint or a cracked solid panel.

By using an oversized corner block, you can add a decorative element to the box, shaping a bead, bevel or roundover into the corner. Also, you can choose to leave the corner block proud of the carcase sides or sand it flush to them.

If you prefer to keep the corner block inconspicuous (flush with the carcase sides), it's better to cut the grooves into the plywood sides and cut tongues in the corner piece to keep the joint strong. That way, the corner block is not weakened by the opposing grooves coming too closely to one another.

Biscuits could also be used to join the corner to the carcase sides. This not only would help align the joint but also would provide a long-grain to long-grain gluing situation.

Mortise and tenon

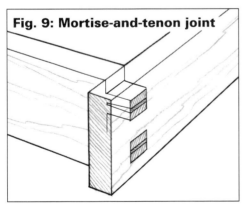

Fig. 9: Mortise-and-tenon joint

Figure 9: Mortise-and-tenon joints can be used to join carcases whenever the sides aren't going to meet flush at a corner. The joint can be hidden or exposed, wedged or not. The joint here, with its hidden wedged-tenon, is a good joint in a situation where strength is needed but the joinery isn't the emphasis.

Mortise-and-tenon joints can be used for carcase construction when the carcase sides are not flush at the corners. An example of this would be a chest of drawers in which the sides are tenoned into mortises in the top.

Mortises can be cut in a variety of ways. Chopping them by hand worked well for a few centuries until someone tried drilling them out first. With a fence on a drill-press table, accurate mortises can be drilled out quickly using a brad-point bit. The corners can then be squared or the tenons pared round to match the mortise.

Plunge routers, however, do a better job with this joint. With an accurate template, you can rout all the mortises at exactly

the right spots to a precisely uniform depth.

An improvement on the mortise and tenon is the addition of a wedge (or wedges) in the tenon. The wedge creates pressure on the walls of the mortise, giving the joint some mechanical strength in addition to the strength of its long-grain glue surface (see figure 9).

If a wedged-tenon is also a through-tenon, as they often are, the wedges add visual interest to the piece as well. It's important, though, that you don't position a wedged-tenon too closely to the end of a board because the short grain on the outboard side of the mortise could easily break.

Finger joints and dovetails

Finger joints and dovetails, because of their large long-grain to long-grain glue surface areas, are the strongest joints in a woodworker's carcase-building repertoire. They are also nice-looking. In terms of appearance, both are best cut in solid stock, though they'd work equally well in plywood.

A tablesaw or router jig is the most efficient means of accurately cutting and spacing finger joints (see figure 10). I use a dado set on my tablesaw with a shop-built jig. A router table also works.

In addition to having a large glue surface area, dovetails also possess a great degree of mechanical strength in one direction. Through- and half-blind (lapped) dovetails are the most commonly used types of dovetails for building carcases.

Through-dovetails can be cut in a variety of ways. Laying them out by hand and using a dovetail saw and chisel is the time-honored approach, but the dovetail-fixture makers are quick to tell you of the ease and speed with which you can achieve perfect results using their products. It's a matter of preference, really, and of how many you'll be cutting. Furnituremakers who cut dovetails daily can cut dovetails for an entire drawer in less time than it takes to read the manual for one of the fixtures. But once you're over the learning curve, it doesn't really take that long to set up one of the fixtures, especially if you have dozens of drawers to dovetail. In either case, make sure the dovetails are well-spaced, ending with half pins at the corners for greatest strength (see figure 11).

Half-blind dovetails are good when you want to hide the joinery from one side, but you still want the strength of dovetails (see figure 12). Drawer fronts are the most obvious example. Done by hand, they require one more marking gauge setup and a bit more chisel work. Regularly spaced half-blind dovetails can also be router cut.

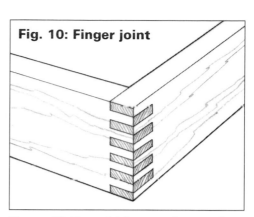

Fig. 10: Finger joint

Figure 10: Finger joints are a strong and attractive way to join a box. The large glue surface area provides a great deal of strength, and the play of light on alternating edge and end grain makes them enticing to look at as well.

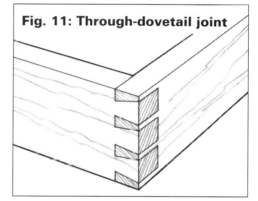

Fig. 11: Through-dovetail joint

Figure 11: Dovetails are the strongest carcase joint and through-dovetails are the simplest dovetails to cut, whether by hand or with a fixture and router. The joint's mechanical strength, large glue surface area and its reputation as being the hallmark of a craftsman make it a perennial favorite even in situations where its strength may not be necessary.

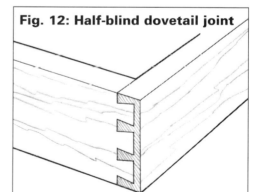

Fig. 12: Half-blind dovetail joint

Figure 12: Half-blind, or lapped, dovetails are a good solution when you need a strong joint but don't want the joinery to steal the show. They're also the classic drawer front-to-side joint, and in contrasting woods, they are very attractive.

Choosing an appropriate joint for a box is as much a matter of personal taste as it is an engineering decision. Boxes in the author's shop include a drawer featuring through- and half-blind dovetails, a simple rabbeted plywood box and three finger-jointed boxes.

DESIGNING FRAME-AND-PANEL DOORS

by Graham Blackburn

Before the advent of frame-and-panel construction, doors (and their owners) were at the mercy of wood movement. Solid plank doors were unruly—likely to split, warp and twist. Subject to expansion and contraction across their entire width, they'd gape open when the weather was dry and swell shut when it was wet. Frame and panel changed all that.

Instead of ignoring or resisting wood movement, frame and panel was designed to accommodate it.

Frame and panel soon became one of the indispensible building blocks of work in solid wood, used not just in doors but in all sorts of case construction and paneling. Over the centuries, the range of its applications has been equalled only by the diversity of stylistic treatments it has received.

Given all this variety, where does a woodworker start when designing frame-and-panel doors? With the structure. It is my feeling that before you can make something look good, you have to be able to make it

Entry door

Queen Anne cupboard

work well. Once you understand why and how frame and panel works, you are halfway to a successful design. In the drawings on the following pages, I've laid out the underpinnings of frame-and-panel construction and followed them with a selection of considerations that inform the design process.

The structural nitty-gritty

The simple genius of the frame-and-panel system is in making a dimensionally stable frame of narrow members and allowing a large solid panel to expand and contract freely inside it. The panel may be large or small, plain or simple, but as long as it is made of solid wood it must be free to move (so that it will not split or buckle with changes in humidity) and at the same time be securely held (so that it cannot warp). Panels are typically held by their edges in grooves formed in the surrounding frame, and they are pinned or glued only at the center.

Occasionally, the grooves are formed by adding a strip of molding to a rabbet, but most often the groove is integral.

The frame members are most commonly mortised and tenoned together, although other methods such as plate joinery or doweling can be used. Because most panels are oriented with their grain running vertically, the rails have the most work to do in preventing the panel from warping. Therefore, the rails are usually the widest parts of the frame. So the frame does not appear top-heavy, the top rail is often made a little narrower than the bottom rail. The stiles are generally made narrower still, giving a pleasing appearance and minimizing the seasonal change in the width of the door.

The proportions of the frame joints may vary depending on the size and function of the piece: More substantial doors should be joined with tenons approximating one-third of the thickness of the members; joints for lighter doors may be a quarter of the thickness.

Purposeful design

Working up the proportions of a door's parts from a structural standpoint will go a long way to producing a pleasing design. But without compromising structural integrity, there remains much you can do to control the final appearance.

You can change the apparent shape of any door by altering the size, shape and number of framing members and reinforce the message with compatible grain patterns. To make an extremely vertical door appear less tall and narrow, for example, try using multiple rails and orienting the grain of the panels horizontally, or make a square door stretch vertically by giving it a number of tall, narrow panels. If you are designing a long, low piece and are concerned it will appear squat and heavy, you can give the piece more lift by dividing the doors so the top panels are smaller than the lower ones.

Control of the focus is another useful design tool. To avoid visual confusion, pick out certain elements of the design for emphasis. For example, you might use plain panels in an unusual frame or surround a strikingly grained panel with a straight-grained frame.

Whatever else is required, design in a style that is in harmony with other woodwork in the room. Even if you don't design in the exact style of the surroundings, try to include elements that will relate, such as elegantly raised panels in a piece destined for a roomful of Colonial furniture or flat panels for a piece that will live with Arts-and-Crafts furniture.

Arts-and-crafts sideboard _____

What's the point of frame and panel?

Solid plank doors are at the mercy of seasonal changes in humidity. Hence, they are unlikely to fit their openings in both summer and winter. Frame and panel solved the problem, making a stable frame and allowing a solid panel to expand and contract inside it.

Plank-and-batten door ignores wood movement

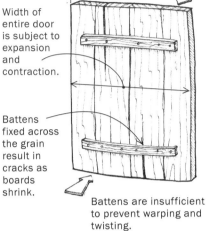

Width of entire door is subject to expansion and contraction.

Battens fixed across the grain result in cracks as boards shrink.

Battens are insufficient to prevent warping and twisting.

Frame-and-panel door accommodates wood movement

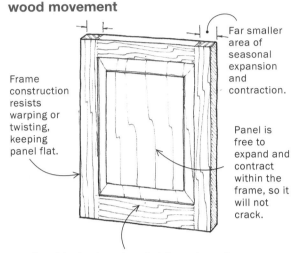

Frame construction resists warping or twisting, keeping panel flat.

Far smaller area of seasonal expansion and contraction.

Panel is free to expand and contract within the frame, so it will not crack.

Panel is glued or pinned at its center only, so dimensional changes occur equally at both sides.

Basic structure of a frame-and-panel door

In a typical frame-and-panel door, the stiles run through from top to bottom, and the grain in the panels is vertical. The rails are generally wider than the stiles, providing wider tenons and better resistance to warping of the panels. One rough rule of thumb suggests that if the bottom rail is one unit wide, the top rail should be two-thirds of a unit wide and the stiles one-half of a unit wide.

When the grain of the panels runs vertically, minimal clearance is needed in rail grooves; more clearance is needed in stile grooves for cross-grain movement.

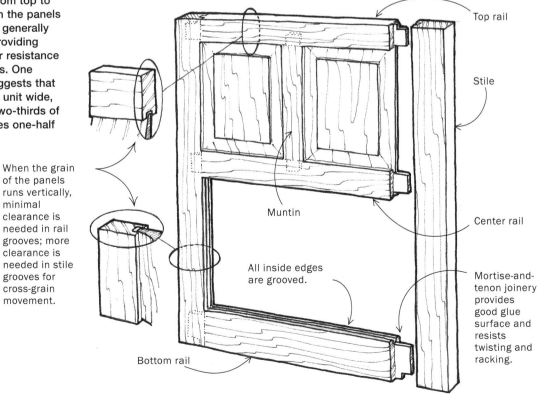

Top rail

Stile

Muntin

Center rail

Mortise-and-tenon joinery provides good glue surface and resists twisting and racking.

All inside edges are grooved.

Bottom rail

Joinery options

Three ways to join the frame

Lighter cabinet doors, especially those with glued-in plywood panels, may be joined with biscuits or dowels.

Mortise and tenon is strongest. The haunch of the tenon increases the joint's resistance to twist.

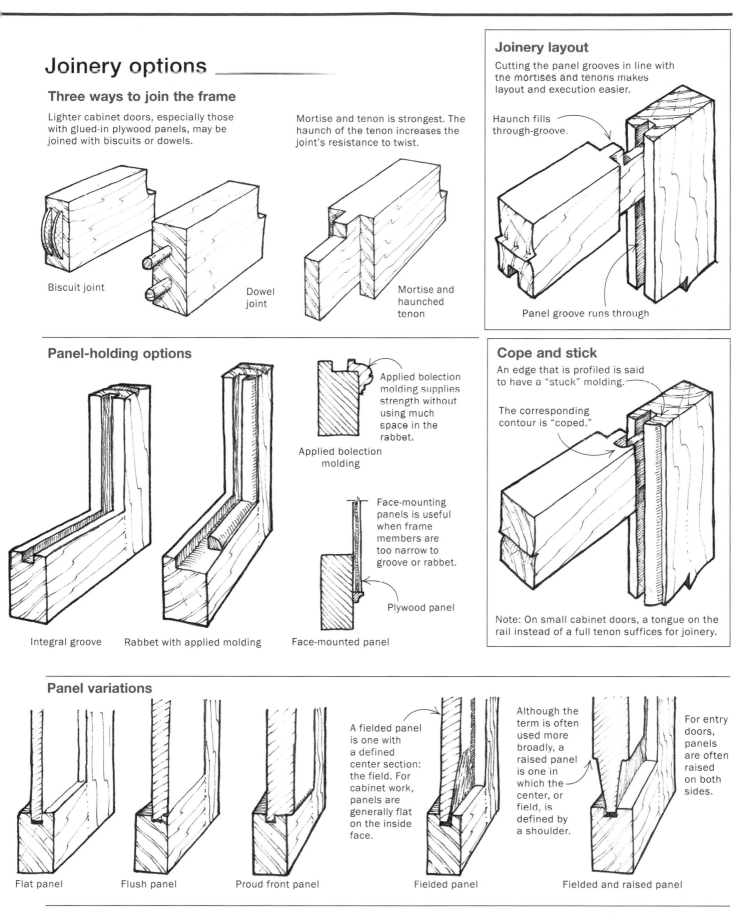

Biscuit joint

Dowel joint

Mortise and haunched tenon

Joinery layout

Cutting the panel grooves in line with the mortises and tenons makes layout and execution easier.

Haunch fills through-groove.

Panel groove runs through

Panel-holding options

Applied bolection molding supplies strength without using much space in the rabbet.

Applied bolection molding

Face-mounting panels is useful when frame members are too narrow to groove or rabbet.

Plywood panel

Integral groove

Rabbet with applied molding

Face-mounted panel

Cope and stick

An edge that is profiled is said to have a "stuck" molding.

The corresponding contour is "coped."

Note: On small cabinet doors, a tongue on the rail instead of a full tenon suffices for joinery.

Panel variations

A fielded panel is one with a defined center section: the field. For cabinet work, panels are generally flat on the inside face.

Although the term is often used more broadly, a raised panel is one in which the center, or field, is defined by a shoulder.

For entry doors, panels are often raised on both sides.

Flat panel

Flush panel

Proud front panel

Fielded panel

Fielded and raised panel

Design: frame-and-panel doors

Working within a given space

Designs for a square opening
Different effects can be achieved for similar spaces by changing the visual focus.

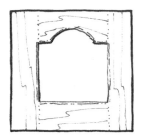

Focus on the framing: Concentrate the shaping on the frame members, and keep the panel neutral in color and pattern.

Focus on the panel: Use dramatic grain matching or veneer within a plain frame.

Stretch the square: Downplay the squareness of the opening by designing a door with strong vertical elements.

Designs for a vertical opening

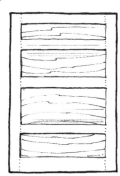

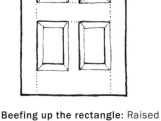

Restate the shape: Keeping the design as simple as possible preserves the essential shape of the opening.

Accentuate the lateral: Introducing strong horizontal elements—three center rails, wide panels with strong grain running side to side—offsets the door's verticality.

Beefing up the rectangle: Raised panels make a door look stronger and heavier; a traditional four-square approach with slightly taller bottom panels provides good balance in a rectangular opening.

Multiple doors for a horizontal space

Stiles at either end of cabinet are made double-wide to balance the paired stiles between. Placing the center rail above the mid-point creates tall lower panels, which give the long, low cabinet a vertical emphasis. For visual balance, the top rail plus the cabinet top equal the width of the bottom rail.

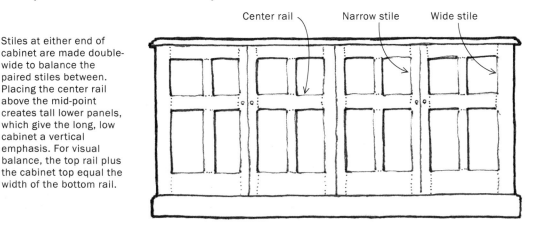

Center rail   Narrow stile   Wide stile

Designing with period styles

Use the characteristics of a period style to design a door in harmony with its surroundings.

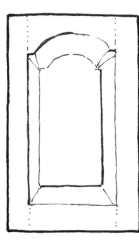

18th century: Classic proportions, raised panels; made of mahogany.

Contemporary: Geometric proportions, unadorned forms; contrasting materials.

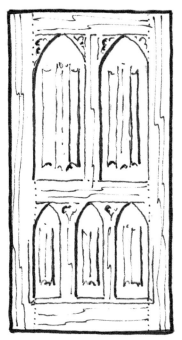

Victorian Gothic: Emphasis on verticality, pointed arch panels, linen-fold carving; polychrome finish or walnut or fumed oak.

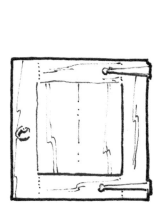

Arts and Crafts: Bold, simple forms, minimal molding, wrought-iron hardware; made of oak.

Proportioning by the book

Although the designer's eye should always be the final judge of what looks good, there are a number of traditional systems you can use to establish pleasing proportions.

Using the golden mean

The golden mean may be expressed as a ratio, BC:AB as AB:AC. This is approximately 5:8.

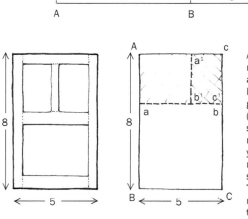

ABCc is a golden rectangle. Squaring a golden rectangle leaves another golden rectangle (shaded area Aabc); squaring this rectangle produces yet another golden rectangle (double-shaded area $a^1b^1c^1c$). This smallest rectangle produced the shape of the door's upper panels.

Using the classical orders of architecture

The Tuscan column (the first of the five classical orders of architecture) is built on a ratio of 1:7. The column width = 1, the column height = 7. All other dimensions are multiples or fractions of this ratio; for example, the base and the capital are each one-half the column width.

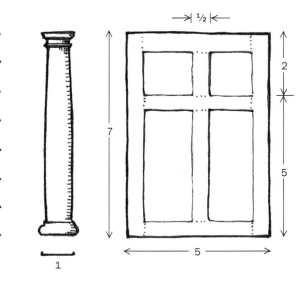

Use the ratio of the Tuscan order (or any other order) to proportion a door. Divide the height of the door by seven, then use multiples or fractions of the resulting unit to size the panels and frame members. (For an 84-in. door, the unit would be 12 in.)

EXPOSING YOUR BACK SIDE

by Christian Becksvoort

A frame-and-raised-panel back makes this cabinet, built by Rick Longenecker of Covington, Ohio, look good from any view. The mortised-and-tenoned frame strengthens the carcase and lets the raised panels expand and contract without affecting the carcase.

The back panel of a lot of case goods is an afterthought, quickly screwed into place before pushing the carcase against a wall where the back is never seen again. But for freestanding pieces or glass-front display cabinets, the back can become the center of attention. When a cabinet back has to play an up-front role, there are a variety of traditional techniques for installing backs that work well. I'll discuss how these techniques have been adapted to contemporary pieces and present an overview of my method of installing a frame-and-panel back.

On display or hidden away, a back serves some important functions. It adds strength and racking resistance, which is most important for open cases and those with adjustable shelves. On closed carcases, the back keeps the contents in and dust, dirt and foreign objects out. When the back is exposed, it should be visually appealing, as shown in the photo on the facing page. And, finally, a back that is square, will automatically square the carcase when it's installed.

Board backs

Traditionally, narrow cabinets often had single board backs. Most often, they were set into rabbets in the sides and top, as shown in the top drawing. Nailed into place, the back provided strength and racking resistance while still allowing the wood to move. Rarely, single board backs were set into grooves in the carcase before assembly. A variation of this type of back, that includes two boards separated by a center stile, is shown in the photo at left on p. 132. Done properly, this method provided a dust-proof, virtually air-tight closure that was also visually attractive. But because space must be left between the carcase and the board to allow for expansion and contraction, this method doesn't provide as much racking resistance for the case.

On wider cabinets, individual boards were joined in a variety of ways, such as shiplap, tongue-and-groove or spline joints (see the bottom drawing). The shiplap is easy to make but has a major drawback: If adjacent boards bow in opposite directions, the joint opens, allowing in dust, dirt and light. Nailing shiplapped boards to a fixed

Back installation

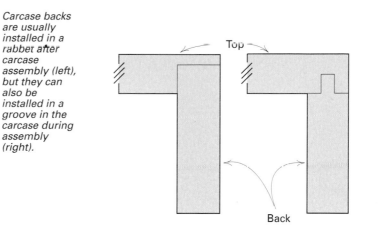

Carcase backs are usually installed in a rabbet after carcase assembly (left), but they can also be installed in a groove in the carcase during assembly (right).

Top

Back

Back panels from individual boards

A variety of interlocking joints can be used when making up a back panel from individual boards.

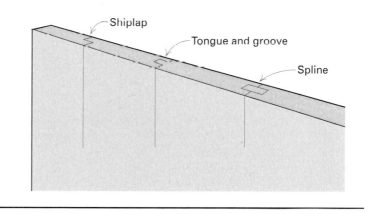

Shiplap

Tongue and groove

Spline

center shelf can overcome this problem, as shown in the photo at right on p. 132. The tongue-and-groove joint solves the problem of warping boards by interlocking the tongue of one board to the groove of its adjacent board. A minor drawback to both the tongue and groove and the shiplap is that they consume $^3/_8$ in. to $^1/_2$ in. of the board's width for the overlap. When making a 4-ft.- or 5-ft.-wide walnut back, this loss to the overlap can prove costly. The spline joint, which is easier to cut than either the shiplap or the tongue and groove, eliminates the waste by butt-joining boards with thin strips that can be ripped from waste.

Whichever method is used, the boards must be allowed to move. They cannot be glued into place but, instead, must be nailed into the rabbet. However, individually nailed boards don't offer much racking resistance and shouldn't be used on large, empty cabinets, especially those without integral face frames.

Plywood backs

Plywood is flat, thin, attractive, has negligible movement and comes in 4x8 sheets. Because it doesn't move, plywood can be glued into rabbets to provide the ultimate in racking resistance. Yet plywood, too, has minor drawbacks. Unless grain direction is irrelevant, it can't be used on pieces wider than 4 ft., and it comes only in a limited variety of species. Also, plywood's thin veneer faces make it difficult to repair nicks, dents and scratches.

Frame-and-panel backs

This brings me to my favorite back, the frame and panel, shown in the photo on p. 134. Built just like a door with stiles, rails and panels, it has all the qualities I require for a back: strength and racking resistance,

A raised panel captured in grooves in the carcase effectively seals the cabinet against dust and light. Although attractive, this type of back doesn't strengthen the carcase as much as a frame glued into a rabbet. (Cabinet built by John Thoe of Seattle, Wash.)

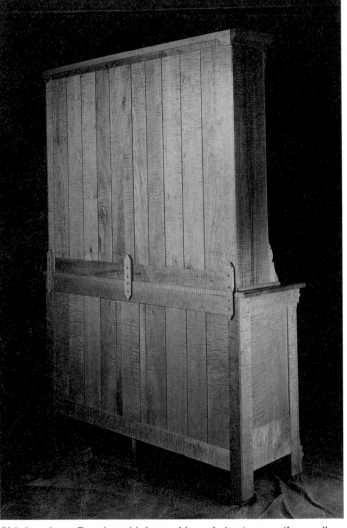

Shiplapping—Framing shiplapped boards is stronger than nailing the boards directly into the back rabbet. Nailing through the boards into a fixed shelf further strengthens the beautiful back on this cabinet built by Ron Layport of Pittsburgh, Pa.

air and dust-tightness, solid-wood construction of the same species as the rest of the cabinet and a pleasing appearance that enhances the overall look of the cabinet. Small cases usually get a single panel frame. Tall cases can have two or three stacked panels. Low, wide pieces may require several side-by-side panels. And large pieces like wardrobes may have stacked and side-by-side panels (see the photo on p. 134).

A frame-and-panel back can include some features of other back styles. For instance, individual boards can be set into a mortised-and-tenoned frame (see the right photo on the facing page). This maintains the look of the traditional, individual-board back while adding to its strength. Another alternative is to use 1/4-in.-thick plywood for the panels. Because the plywood is recessed into the frame, the panel is protected from most nicks and scratches.

But I prefer to use solid-wood panels in frames. This gives me the most flexibility regarding the species of wood used as well as the style of the panel. Like doors, backs can have a variety of panel styles to suit the style of the cabinet, as shown in the bottom drawing at right. Although my first choice is usually a flush panel, I've used several different panel styles. Other options include 1/4-in.-thick, solid flat panels, a variety of raised-panel styles or combination panels with a flat face on the interior and a raised panel face on the exterior. Non-wood materials, such as stained or translucent glass, melamine, slate or composition panels covered with leather or velvet, also can be used for panels.

Building a frame

I like to use 5/8-in.-thick stock for the frames in all but the smallest cases. This thickness represents a good compromise between strength and weight. Frames 3/4 in. thick add too much weight, especially on large cases, and 1/2-in.-thick frames yield weak mortise-and-tenon joints. I use narrow, quartersawn stock for the frame members to reduce wood movement.

Quartersawn stock moves roughly half as much as plainsawn stock. By keeping the

Mortised-and-tenoned back frame

A mortised-and-tenoned back frame adds strength and racking resistance to backs made up of individual boards or solid panels and accommodates wood movement.

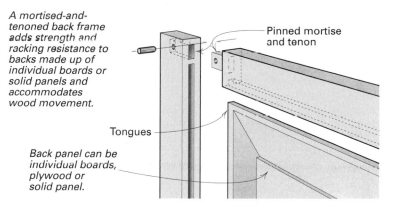

Pinned mortise and tenon

Tongues

Back panel can be individual boards, plywood or solid panel.

Back panel options

Back can take a variety of forms to suit the cabinet style.

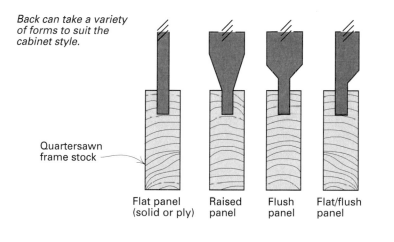

Quartersawn frame stock

Flat panel (solid or ply)   Raised panel   Flush panel   Flat/flush panel

frame members 1 1/4 in. to 1 3/4 in. wide, the overall movement is limited to under 3/64 in. (for quartersawn cherry) no matter how wide the back. This amount of movement is easily handled by the compression of the wood fibers and will not push apart the carcase or break the rabbet joint.

If the bottom rail of the frame is not captured in a rabbet, as shown in the photo below, it, like all other secondary stiles and rails, can be made as wide as desired. A wider bottom rail allows larger mortise-and-tenon joints and makes a stronger back frame. The mortises and tenons are glued and pinned, but the panels are free to float

A frame-and-panel back with flush panels is built like a door with stiles, rails and panels and is glued into a rabbet in the carcase. It provides racking resistance and keeps dust and air out.

in the frame grooves. A loose wood panel can be anchored to prevent it from rattling in the groove. Center the panel in its frame, and then drive a 20-gauge brad through the frame and the panel tongue, centered at both the top and bottom of the panel.

Installing the back panel

Before installing the assembled back frame and panel into its rabbet in the completed carcase, I trim the panel assembly square to fit snugly into the rabbet, using the table-saw, jointer and a block plane. The carcase rabbet should be $1/32$ in. deeper than the thickness of the back because it is easier to trim the back edge of the carcase flush with the back panel than to sand the entire back panel flush with the sides. To make it easier to slide the back frame into the rabbet, I chamfer the edge along the inside face of the frame with the block plane. I also mark the locations of all the carcase's fixed dividers and shelves and the bottom, so I can nail through the back frame into these components to further strengthen the carcase. Just prior to installation, I sand the back panel to 320-grit on the inside face and ease all the sharp edges.

Finally, I glue the back into place, spreading glue thinly on both faces of the rabbet as well as the edge of the back. After forcing the back into the rabbet, I clamp top to bottom first and then side to side. There should be no gaps between the back frame and the rabbet. Because the back has been squared, it will automatically correct a minor out-of-square carcase as the back is clamped into place. When the glue is dry, I remove the clamps, drill holes at the previously marked dividers, shelves and bottom and nail the back with 4d finishing nails. I countersink the nails about $1/4$ in. and then plug the hole with small, $1/8$-in.-sq. pegs of the same species wood as the carcase. I trim the end-grain plugs flush, plane the carcase flush to the back, sand the entire back to 320-grit and, again, ease all frame and panel edges.

FACE FRAME OPTIONS FOR PLYWOOD CABINETS

by Joseph Beals

One of the first face frames I built was a nightmare at every step. It was a maple behemoth, more than 11 ft. long, for a row of cabinets I had built at the job site. When I glued up the frame in my shop, the dowel joints would not line up until I fairly beat them together. I applied the finished frame on-site just as a thunderstorm blew in. I spread white glue on the back of the frame and used two hands, two knees and my forehead to hold it in place. A lightning bolt took out the power at about the third nail. As I set the frame by kerosene lamp, I decided face frames must be the nastiest job invented.

Face frames complete a cabinet. The author fits a face frame to a plywood carcase, giving the cabinet the appearance of solid-wood furniture.

Guidelines for designing face frames

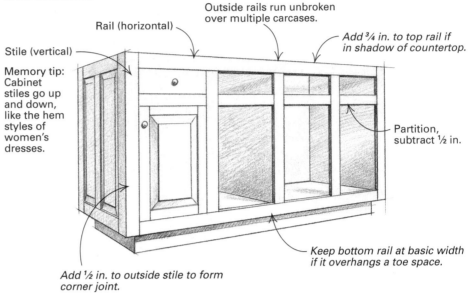

Start with a basic width of 1¾ in. for rails, stiles and partitions, and vary it according to the rules below.

Rail (horizontal)

Outside rails run unbroken over multiple carcases.

Stile (vertical)

Add ¾ in. to top rail if in shadow of countertop.

Memory tip: Cabinet stiles go up and down, like the hem styles of women's dresses.

Partition, subtract ½ in.

Keep bottom rail at basic width if it overhangs a toe space.

Add ½ in. to outside stile to form corner joint.

I have made plenty of face frames since then, and they don't seem nearly as difficult anymore. I now make them with mortise-and-tenon joints and attach them to carcases with biscuits or with counterbored and plugged screws.

How a face frame is made is no more important than how it's designed. Face frames should be a subtle element in the composition of a cabinet. A face frame that draws attention to itself through awkward proportions or wild grain isn't doing its job.

And no matter how face frames are made, they all do the same thing. A solid-wood face frame provides a finished front on casework that's usually made of some manufactured material such as plywood or fiberboard. The frame covers the raw edges, provides a place to hang doors, fit drawers and attach trim. Face frames are appropriate for a variety of practical, built-in and free-standing furniture.

Design face frames like doors

Parts of a face frame are best put together as if they were a conventional door frame:

Outer stiles should run full height, with top and bottom rails let in between. Internal partitions should follow the same pattern (see the drawing above).

These rules serve well in most instances, but they should be modified when a pair of face frames are joined end to end. The joint between them will look best if the top and bottom rails butt into each other, rather than into side-by-side stiles. This will give the illusion of a continuous frame, which looks better.

It's important to use straight-grained, stable stock for face frames. Wild grain should be avoided, even when the rail or stile is fastened along its length, such as along a cabinet bottom. It will draw the eye to a pattern that probably has no symmetry or other resolution. The frame should not compete visually with the doors and drawers it surrounds.

There are no best dimensions for the various rails, stiles and partitions, just some guidelines to keep them visually balanced. I mill rough 4/4 stock to $^{13}/_{16}$ in., but standard $^3/_4$-in. stock is fine. The parts should be neither so wide as to appear clumsy nor so narrow as to seem fragile. The proportions of smaller parts such as drawer partitions should be reduced to keep them from looking oversized. For a face frame that will house flush-mounted doors and drawers, I find 1³/₄ in. to be the most satisfying width for ordinary stiles, and I derive other component dimensions from it.

Outside stiles need to be wider at corners because they form a joint. To make both appear 1³/₄ in. wide and maintain symmetry around the corner, one must be cut down to 1 in. wide or less. Working with such a narrow piece is not worth the effort, especially if grooved for a panel. I widen the front stile to 2¹/₄ in. and make the side stile 1¹/₂ in. wide. (For more on how to get around a corner, see the box on p. 143.)

You have several assembly choices

There are at least four ways to make a face frame: with dowels, biscuits, pocket screws or more traditional mortise-and-tenon joinery. Your choice will probably depend on what tools you have on hand and which method you have experience with. For me, the best approach is the old-fashioned way—the mortise and tenon—even if it takes a little longer and is a little more complicated. (The first three methods are explained in more detail on p. 138.)

Mortise-and-tenon joints are strong, very reliable and easily made. They give positive, foolproof alignment of parts. To cut mortises, I use a small slot mortising machine. You could use a router, which is also very fast and accurate.

I make the mortises about ³/₈ in. deep and about ⁵/₁₆ in. wide. It's not necessary to make them deeper because a face frame is not subject to particularly severe loading. They should be easy to put together but without too much play (see the photos showing my approach on pp. 140-142).

When all the joints have been cut, I dry-fit the face frame and compare it to measurements on my drawings and the carcase. It helps to imagine the finished cabinet and overlay that mental picture on the face frame, in case something brutally obvious has slipped through the design process. If all is well, I glue it together.

I brush yellow glue in the mortises and on the tenons and fit the frame together across sawhorses (see the bottom photo on p. 140). I clamp across all joints with just enough pressure to bring the tenon shoulders home tight, checking once again to make sure the joints are flat. Adjustments can be made by shifting a clamp or moving it to the opposite side. However, unlike a door, a face frame does not need to be perfectly flat. Because it's relatively thin, the frame will be fairly limber and will be drawn flat when fitted to the carcase. I also check each joint for square and lateral alignment, adjusting them with a hammer and block if necessary.

I measure diagonals to check the face frame for square (see the photo on p. 141). This is crucial, but easy to forget. To square a slightly racked face frame, I skew each clamp slightly. If that doesn't work, I add a clamp across the long diagonal to pull it into place. Despite every care, the square of the door and drawer openings on a complex face frame may not agree with the overall squareness of the frame. When this happens, I split the difference.

Attach face frame to carcases

Whenever possible, I attach the face frame in my shop because all my tools are nearby, and clamping a frame to a cabinet is much easier when the cabinet can be parked on a couple of sawhorses. Attaching them on-site is an option if the carcases and frames are too big to carry as a single unit. Attaching a face frame to carcases after they've been set in place is my last option, though there are circumstances when it's the best method.

No matter where you end up attaching face frames, the single most demanding detail is keeping the top edge of the bottom rail flush with the inside of the cabinet bottom. (One exception is when the cabinet bottom becomes a door stop.) The veneers on most cabinet-grade plywoods are very thin and will not withstand much planing or sanding. The top edge of the bottom rail must, therefore, be fastened dead flush or a fraction proud to permit finishing to a smooth joint. This joint has always been particularly important to me. I think it's a sign of sloppy work when it's not flush, but others may not be so obsessed.

Three common ways to build a frame

Face frame joints don't need to be particularly strong, but they should go together easily and be simple to align. Mortise-and-tenon joinery is traditional (see a description of my approach on pp. 140-142), but face frames can also be assembled with dowels, biscuits or pocket screws.

Dowels

Pros: Doweled face frames are easy to lay out because you don't need to figure in tenon lengths.

Cons: To prevent frame pieces from rotating, each joint requires two dowels, which can be difficult to align accurately. Once drilled, dowel holes can't be adjusted to compensate for even the smallest alignment mistakes during assembly. If used with yellow glue, doweled joints must be pressed tight at one go: a lapse of a minute or less will let a dowel seize with the joint open.

Biscuits

Pros: Biscuit joints are the fastest and easiest joint to make. They align quickly and positively.

Cons: Kerfs for the smallest standard-sized biscuit will break through and show on edges of stock narrower than $2\frac{3}{8}$ in. If a molding detail will be added to the inside of the face frame, biscuits may be the most convenient joinery choice.

Pocket screws

Pros: Pocket screws on the back of the frame make a fast and simple joint.

Cons: Joints are difficult to align perfectly flat and can't be adjusted in any practical manner during assembly without pulling out screws. A dedicated jig is needed to drill screw holes.

Attaching frames on the job site

It's often easier to apply face frames while cabinets are still in the shop, but very large or long cabinets are a different story. When a number of smaller cabinet components are put together on a job site, they can be joined with a common face frame. In that situation, frames can be attached to the cabinets with screws or nails.

Plugged screws

Pros: Plugged screws are useful when clamping a biscuit joint is not an option. They are the equal of biscuits for strength and overall convenience, and can be used with biscuits for better alignment. Use $1\frac{5}{8}$-in. black drywall screws through a $\frac{13}{16}$-in.-thick face frame. They grip well in plywood and do not require a pilot hole.

Cons: The plugs show if the cabinet is finished bright.

Nails

Pros: The oldest and simplest method is glue and nails, especially for painted work. Nail holes are small and can be filled easily.

Cons: Nails will sometimes wander sideways in a plywood edge, shifting the face frame. Occasionally, a nail will split the plywood or pop out of a cabinet side. Nailed frames are difficult to align exactly without biscuits.

My way of making face frames

Use mortise-and-tenon joinery for a strong, easily aligned joint. To save time, cut the tenon shoulders on the tablesaw without changing the blade height.

Before glue-up, dry-fit the whole frame. This ensures all pieces will go together smoothly when coping with glue that sets quickly and an armload of clamps.

Sawhorses make clamping up easy. They'll let you fit clamps on both sides of the frame for even clamping pressure.

Shop installation with biscuits and clamps
When I attach face frames in the shop, I use biscuits almost exclusively (see the top photo on p. 142). The biscuit joint is strong, accurate and doesn't show. Also, biscuits are invaluable along the bottom rail, which demands accurate positioning. However, it's foolish to trust the biscuit to align everything perfectly because there can be some occasional play in the slots. Even

with biscuits, you should expect to make adjustments.

In some materials, such as medium-density fiberboard, biscuits may be the only practical attachment because screws hold poorly in the edge and tend to split the material. Although biscuits allow me to eliminate screws entirely, the disadvantage is that I need to use clamps (see the bottom photo on p. 142). Clamps tie up the carcase

Only perfect rectangles have equal diagonals. The author compares diagonals to make sure the face frame is square. Angling the clamps corrects minor problems.

Biscuits are best. Although strong, biscuits can be difficult to align when the face frame hangs over the edge of the cabinet. Instead of resetting the fence on his biscuit joiner, the author uses a spacer block the thickness of the overhang to align the tool.

Clamp-up is a cinch with the carcase on its back. Face frames attached with biscuits need to be clamped. Sawhorses make it easy to reach all the edges of the carcase and face frame.

for at least an hour, and they always get in the way of cleaning off glue that squeezes out of the joints.

On-site installation with plugged screws

For a very long run of cabinets, on-site installation of face frames has some benefits. Long runs of cabinets look better when united with a single face frame, but attaching them all in the shop and moving them

to the site later is impractical. Multiple cabinets should be set in place individually, then fastened together to ensure they're square, plumb and aligned.

Shop installation of face frames is convenient because the cabinets can lie on their backs, which gives full access for clamping. On-site, after the cabinets are set against the walls, clamping access disappears. In this application, counterbored, plugged screws

Turning a corner

As seen from the top, face frames can be joined at a cabinet corner in several ways.

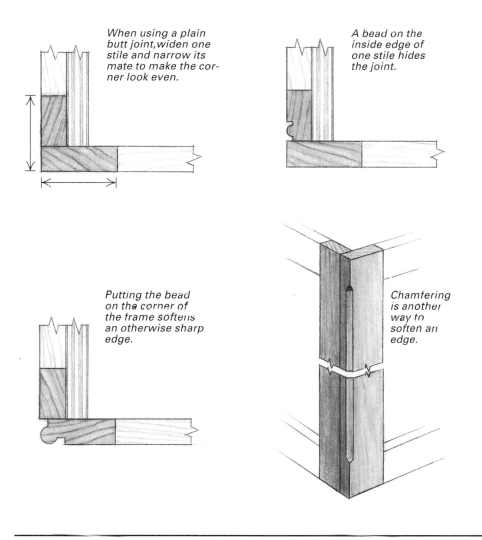

When using a plain butt joint, widen one stile and narrow its mate to make the corner look even.

A bead on the inside edge of one stile hides the joint.

Putting the bead on the corner of the frame softens an otherwise sharp edge.

Chamfering is another way to soften an edge.

are hard to match for strength and overall convenience. Once they're in, the attachment is done. Screws grip well in plywood and do not require a pilot hole in the plywood edge.

To hide the screws, I use plugs cut from the same stock as the face frame. For bright finished work, I try to match grain pattern and color as well. After the glue dries, I strike off most of the excess plug with a chisel and watch how the grain runs. If the grain runs down into the plug, some of the plug can pop off below the surface, leaving a

tedious repair job. To avoid it, I finish paring off the plug from the other direction.

Plugged holes vanish under paint, but even with careful grain and color matching, that little circle is always visible under a bright finish. This isn't necessarily offensive, but it requires that screw holes be carefully and symmetrically aligned. I find that there is something pleasing about a thoughtful, geometric pattern of plugs along the edges of a face frame.

MAKING BIG CABINETS MANAGEABLE

by Niall Barrett

Working in New York City, where most of my clients live, is trying even at the best of times. There's rarely ever a place to park, so I end up double-parking to unload a delivery, always keeping a sharp eye out for the police. After that, I'm forced to pay exorbitant fees to park my van in a lot. Freight elevators tend to be small and poorly located, and stairways have sharp corners to negotiate. I once delivered a cabinet that would not fit in the elevator, so I had to walk it up two flights of stairs. I was lucky the client didn't live on the 35th floor.

Doors and hallways can be quite narrow when you're trying to deliver a large cabinet.

These anxiety-provoking restrictions and horror stories from fellow cabinetmakers are what started me thinking about cabinets in a new way. It became clear to me that smaller parts were the answer. They would be easier to handle and transport. The challenge would be to assemble them quickly and not have the end result look like a jigsaw puzzle of small pieces. These days, I routinely build large pieces, like the stand-alone television cabinet shown above, in easily handled components. When I get to a job site, whether it's in New York City or elsewhere, I assemble the pieces with knockdown hardware.

This approach is not just for woodworkers who make deliveries to a large city. It also works for the guy building a large pantry cabinet in his garage who will have to move it through the house into the kitchen.

Make cabinets easy to finish and move

Small components are light and easy to move around the workroom and take up less space at every step of the way. For me, that's important because I work in a fairly small shop in the basement of my house. The ceilings are less than 8 ft. off the floor. I often build units that are too large to put together in my shop; they aren't fully assembled until they are delivered to the site.

Whether you use stain, oil, varnish or a sprayed lacquer topcoat, finishes are easy to apply when you work with small components and flat panels. There are no corners to collect excess stain, primer or topcoat, so the finish looks more even. Also, by working with flat panels, you can get a lot more finishing done by spraying pieces vertically. They take up less floor space than finished cabinets, so I can spray more at one time. And by spraying flat panels vertically, they collect less dust as they dry. This can be significant because I usually use a water-based finish, which takes longer to dry than nitrocellulose lacquer.

Television cabinet, one piece at a time

For author Niall Barrett, getting a new custom cabinet from his shop in upstate New York to a client's house many miles away is all in a day's work. Many of the cabinets he makes, like the television cabinet in the photos at left, go in pieces and are assembled on the spot with knock-down hardware. Parts for the cabinet easily fit inside a standard minivan (facing page).

At the site, the author sets the base (1), adds two lower carcases (2), attaches finished side pieces (3) and, finally, adds the top, door and hardware (4). Elapsed time is approximately four hours.

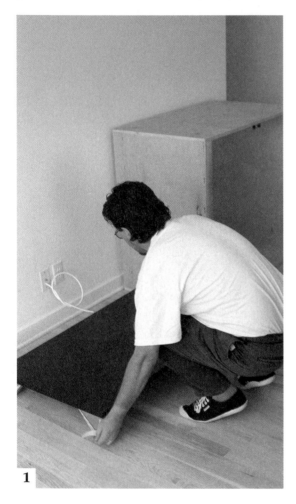

1

2

You can fit an incredibly large volume of material into a small truck or van if the project is broken down into flat or small pieces (see the photo on p. 144). This alone can save a few hundred dollars for the rental of a large truck and the time it takes to pick it up and return it. Oh yes, the other benefit I enjoy is the amazed look on the client's face after the collection of parts I delivered is almost magically transformed into a beautiful piece of furniture.

Plan ahead for components and fasteners

When I'm in the design phase, I start by thinking about how a piece can be broken down into smaller, more manageable parts and how I'll put it together again. I determine, for example, whether a cabinet with a center divider and two doors can be made as two cabinets. Or I'll weigh the advantages of making the crown and the base as separate components rather than permanently fastening them to the case in the shop. I make a quick sketch, an exploded view of

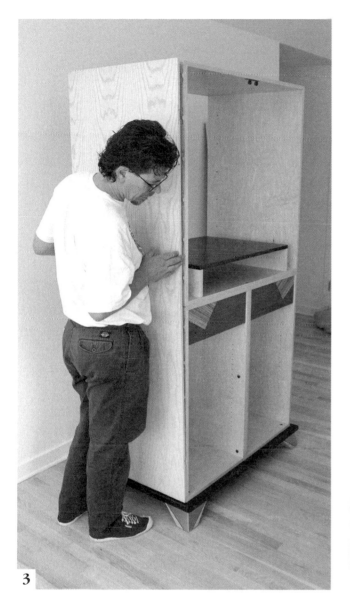

3

4

the individual parts, to see whether it makes sense to build something that way. Detailed drawings can follow later.

Once I've determined which route to take, I think about design elements that make the job go more smoothly and the piece look better when it's done. Knockdown hardware makes strong connections between cabinet parts, but it can be difficult to make two surfaces align perfectly along the length of a joint. To solve this problem, I sometimes add a spacer between cabinets and set it back slightly from the

edge. This creates a shadow line at the joint and makes the seam less obvious. For the same reason, it's usually better to offset one hard surface from another, like the seam where a bed rail joins the corner post.

No matter how you decide to break a job into smaller pieces, the trick is putting it all together so it looks like a unified whole. And that's where the hardware shown on pp. 148-149 comes in.

Knockdown fasteners for small components

Knockdown hardware offers the strength and durability of more permanent fasteners but allows a cabinet to be taken apart and moved as easily as it was assembled. There are many types of knockdown, or ready-to-assemble, hardware. Here are the author's favorites.

Hex-drive connector bolts

These are bolts with a machine thread, usually ¼-20, and large, flat heads that you tighten with an Allen wrench (see the top photos below). I team them up with threaded inserts for right-angle joints, shelves and dividers. I also use the inserts to attach crown and base assemblies to cabinet cases.

These bolts also come with matching threaded sleeves. I use them for fastening the sides of two cabinet carcases to one another (see the bottom photos below). The standard finish is an antique bronze color. But you can also buy these bolts in black, or you can spray paint them any color that you like. A number of suppliers sell these bolts and sleeves. I usually buy mine at either Woodcraft (800-225-1153) or Liberty Hardware (800-542-3789).

Lamello Simplex KD fasteners

These fasteners come as interlocking aluminum parts to be glued into regular biscuit slots. They are used in pairs. I often use this hardware to join flat pieces edge to edge and at 90° angles to one another. The hardware is invisible once installed. I used them to join the finished side panels over the cabinet carcases in the installation shown in the top far right photo on the facing page.

Epoxy glue works best for installation, although I have had some success using polyurethane glue for light applications where the joint is not under much stress from weight or tension. Lamello makes a tool intended to simplify installation. I buy the fasteners and the insertion tool from Select Machinery (800-789-2323).

Hex-drive connector bolts and threaded inserts fasten cabinet parts together where connector heads can be exposed. The connector at right secures a cabinet carcase to its base.

Hex-drive connector bolts and threaded sleeves—This hardware is ideal for linking adjoining carcases.

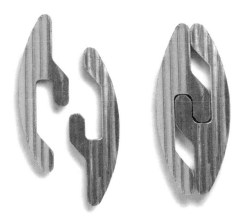

Lamello Simplex fasteners are one option when hardware must be hidden. These are ideal for attaching a finished face piece to a cabinet side (right).

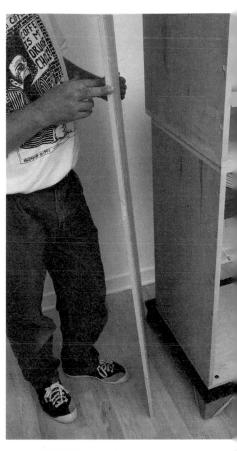

Confirmat connecting screws

These connecting screws (see the photos below) have a deep thread with no taper. To use them, you must also buy a special step drill bit for piloting the workpieces, as shown in the bottom photo at right. You can use these screws to put a cabinet together and to take it apart again a number of times with no loss of holding power. You can buy these screws with small heads, designed to be countersunk, or with large, flat heads like those of hex-drive connector bolts. I only use those with small heads.

Also, you need a special driver bit called a Pozidrive. It looks a lot like a standard Phillips head, but it fits and grabs better in the head of the screw. A Phillips bit will strip the head of the screw if you drive it home with a lot of torque. Outwater Hardware (800-631-0342) sells the screws and bits.

Confirmat screws can be inserted and removed many times without sacrificing holding power. They require a special bit and driver.

SHELF SUPPORT OPTIONS

by Stephen Winchester

I earn my living by making cabinetry—not cookie-cutter kitchens, but one-of-a-kind pieces and custom built-ins. Every cabinet I build has at least one shelf. And some—hutches and book cabinets, for example—have many. As both designer and fabricator in most cases, I try to balance style, function and cost when figuring out how to support shelves in a cabinet.

Over the years, I have come to favor several techniques that achieve that happy balance between elegance and efficiency (the five methods I use most often are described on the following pages). My methods aren't as crude as using stamped-steel brackets but neither are they as fussy as routing tapered sliding dovetails.

Fixed or adjustable shelving

Style of cabinetry is the most important factor in determining which of the methods of shelving support I use. The next most important factor is cost. For cabinets in kitchens, pantries and utility rooms, fixed shelves are generally fine (see the story on the facing page). But for most of my work, clients want adjustable shelves. Shelf standards, long vertical tracks that go into a case's sides, are the most visible and utilitarian-looking, but they're also the quickest to install (see the story on p. 152). Drilling holes in the side of the case for shelf pins is the next quickest (see the story on p. 153). Another technique employs what I call invisible wires that slip into thin kerfs in the ends of the shelves (see the story on p. 154). And there are sawtooth supports, which are quite elegant, but relatively time-consuming (see the story on p. 155). The more complicated the method, the more I have to charge.

As far as function goes, any of these supports will hold a reasonable load: 3 ft. of books shouldn't be a problem. Even the thin, invisible wires have a tremendous amount of shear strength.

In the rare instances I've made shelves longer than 36 in., I've used a strongback, which is a wooden reinforcing bar either beneath or at the front of a shelf. Even with a strongback, though, I wouldn't plan to stack 4 ft. of encyclopedias on an otherwise unsupported shelf.

Blind-nailed dado

Here in New Hampshire, painted pine cupboards are popular. They're a frequent choice for kitchen cabinets, where one or two shelves are all that's necessary. These shelves can be fixed at standard intervals to allow for stacks of plates and glasses. For these shelves, I use a blind-nailed dado (see the drawing at right). It's quick, and the shelves are strong and look neat.

Because my clients like the look of handplaned boards, I plane the sides, top, bottom and shelves of the cupboards after taking them to thickness with my planer. Then I cut the shelf stock ¾ in. longer than the inside measurement of the cabinet (this allows for a ⅜-in. dado in each upright) and mark the dadoes directly from the ends of the shelves, using a sharp knife. I also number everything so that if the shelves vary slightly in thickness, they will still fit their dadoes snugly.

I remove the waste with the radial-arm saw, using a dado set that's slightly smaller than the width of the finished slot. I take two passes and cut just to the scored line on each side. Shelves are installed as the case is assembled. Then I drill for the nails to avoid splitting the stock. I use 6d box or finish nails and take care not to drive one through the side of the cabinet. With the box nails, I hammer the heads flat on the sides, so they look more like a cut nail.

These cabinets are of a traditional style, so I usually attach a face frame to their front edges. If you want a frameless, more contemporary-looking cabinet, you could stop the dadoes shy of the front of the cabinet, square them up and have blind dadoes.

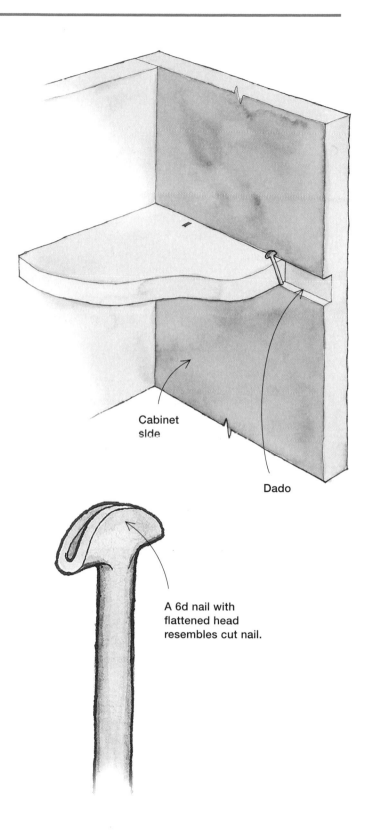

Cabinet side

Dado

A 6d nail with flattened head resembles cut nail.

Shelf standards

Shelf standards are the quickest, simplest way of installing adjustable shelving (see the drawing). They're not, however, the most attractive. Still, there are situations where they're the perfect solution, and they can be painted to match the cabinet. The spacing between holes for the clips is ½ in., so standards are the most adjustable of the methods I use.

To install the standards, I plow a dado ⅝ in. wide and ³⁄₁₆ in. deep all the way from the top to the bottom of the cabinet sides. Then I assemble the cabinet, finish it and nail the standards in, paying attention to which end of the standard is up.

I nail the standards to the cabinet sides with the special nails that come with the standards. If cabinets are going to be placed next to each other, make sure they don't share a side (each case needs to have its own wall), or the nails will hit each other.

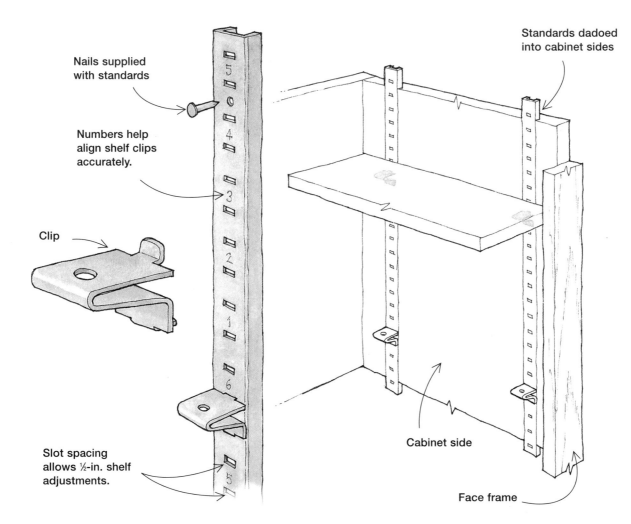

Nails supplied with standards

Numbers help align shelf clips accurately.

Clip

Slot spacing allows ½-in. shelf adjustments.

Standards dadoed into cabinet sides

Cabinet side

Face frame

Shelf pins

I like shelf pins because they're quick and easy to install (see the photos), very little hardware shows and, depending on how closely the holes are spaced, they're almost infinitely adjustable. Spacing the holes 1 in. on center works out about right. I also set the row of holes 1½ in. from the edges of the case sides. I drill the holes using a shopmade template before assembling the cabinet. I measure for the shelves after assembly.

Pins are available in a number of different shapes, sizes and materials, including plastic, plated steel and brass.

You can even get pins with rubber cushions for use with glass shelving. The most common sizes are 5mm and ¼ in. And if you don't like the look of commercial pins, you can always whittle your own.

I don't need to drill holes all the way from the top to the bottom of the sides. I figure out the minimum and maximum spacing I'd like between shelves. Then I lay out lines on the case sides reflecting those parameters. For example, I never drill holes closer than 5 in. from the top or bottom of a case because a shelf that close generally wouldn't be useful.

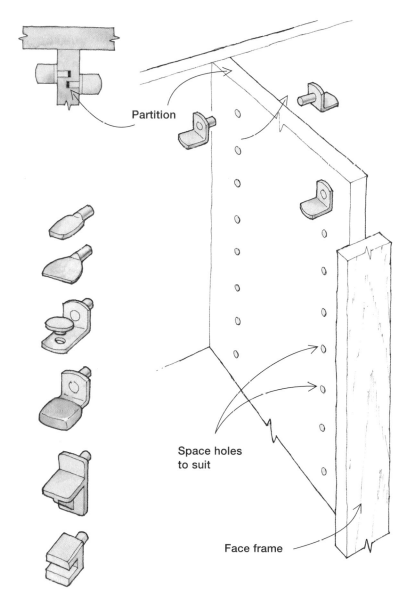

Partition

Space holes to suit

Face frame

Drilling shelf-pin holes. A template with an end-stop positions the template accurately top to bottom and eliminates the possibility of measuring errors (below).

A gauge block ensures a consistent setback from the edge of the case. Different-width gauge blocks can be used for special applications, such as drilling offset pin holes from both sides of one upright (photo top right and drawing at left). A wooden stop block sets the depth (right). It won't move either, like many metal collars. Blue masking tape indicates where the holes in the case sides should stop.

Invisible wires

This method is pretty slick and looks great on more contemporary, frameless cabinetry. The only thing that will show on a cabinet with shelves supported by these "invisible" wires is a series of ⅛-in. holes. No hardware is visible at all. But because the shelves slide onto the wires, you can't use them on cabinets that have face frames (see the drawing).

It's nearly as easy to cut, bend and install invisible wires as it is to install shelf pins. If I have a bunch of cabinets to do, I make a template, just as I do for shelf pins. If I only have a few to do, I use a marking gauge and a tape measure to lay out the hole centers.

I use suspended-ceiling wire (available from most home centers and large lumberyards) for the supports. It's about ⅛ in. dia., and a 10 ft. length costs less than $2. In a pinch, coat-hanger wire could be used. I measure the diameter of the wire with a caliper and then choose a bit to match. I also drill a test hole to make sure the wire fits snugly but not so tightly that it has to be pounded in.

I snip the wire to length with a pair of lineman's pliers and bend the wires in a vise. To get the wire to bend in the right place,

I position it so the mark indicating the bend is just above the vise jaws. I bend it by hand first and then tap the corner flat with a hammer. Blind slots for the wires are cut in the ends of each shelf on the tablesaw but are stopped ¼ in. shy of the front edge of each shelf. I use a standard-kerf blade, but if you use a thin-kerf blade, just make two passes. The slots are centered on the ends of the shelves.

Installing wire supports. Drill the holes about ⅝ in. deep (top left). Masking tape is an effective depth gauge. Cut the wire to length, and mark it for bending (top right). The wire should be as long as the distance between the holes plus 2½ in.—twice the depth of the holes and twice the amount of wire sticking out before it bends. To bend the wire, put it in the vise, push it over by hand and tap it flat with a hammer (bottom left). Check for consistency (bottom right). Wires should protrude about ⅝ in. from each hole. Trim if necessary.

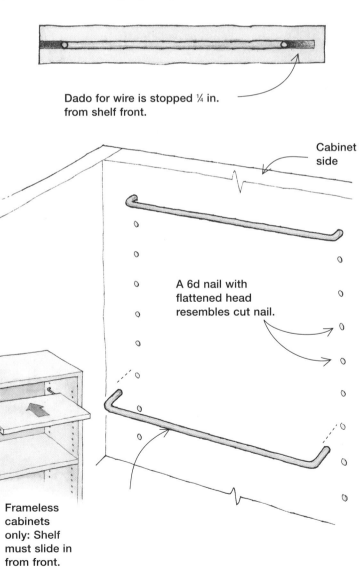

Dado for wire is stopped ¼ in. from shelf front.

Cabinet side

A 6d nail with flattened head resembles cut nail.

Frameless cabinets only: Shelf must slide in from front.

Sawtooth supports

I've saved the best-looking shelf supports for last. They're not difficult to make—just a little time-consuming (see the photos).

After milling stock for the sawtooth supports and the cleats that go between them (both are the same dimensions, about ⅜ in. to ½ in. thick and 1¼ in. wide), I mark the four uprights from a sawtooth pattern. Then I saw them out together on the radial-arm saw and the bandsaw.

I clean up sawmarks with a chisel and glue and nail the sawtoothed strips to the carcase sides at the front and rear. Cleats span the distance between supports; the shelves are notched around them.

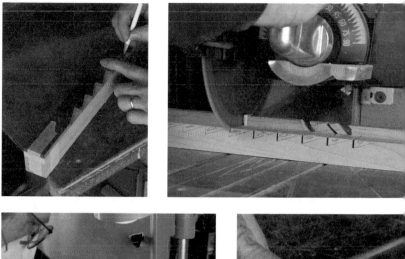

Making sawtooth supports. Mark out sawtooth patterns on the dimensioned stock (top left). A pattern made from ¼-in. hardboard speeds layout. Tape the four uprights together, and then tape the pattern to the stack to keep the pattern in place. Cut the straight part of the sawtooth on the radial-arm saw or tablesaw (top right). Bandsaw the angled part of the sawtooth (bottom left). Then pare the faces of the sawteeth smooth, and clean out the corners (bottom right).

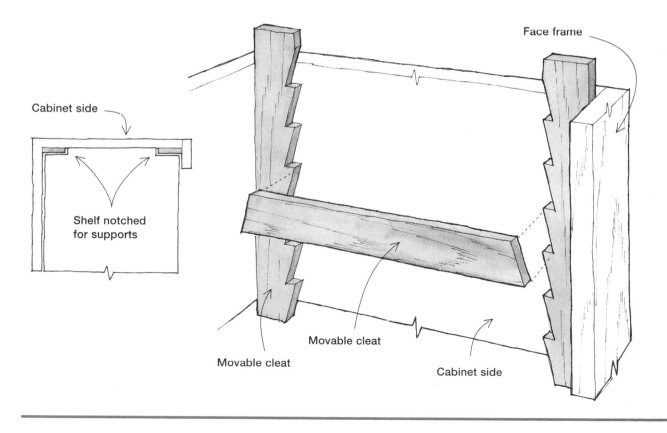

Cabinet side

Shelf notched for supports

Face frame

Movable cleat

Movable cleat

Cabinet side

KEEPING DOORS CLOSED

by Christian H. Becksvoort

A handsome cabinet door, hung precisely in its frame, is a pleasure to use. But the door isn't quite finished until it's been fitted with a proper catch. There sure are plenty of choices, from simple turn buttons to elaborate library catches. The hard part is picking the catch that's appropriate. What's appropriate? A catch that is in keeping with the period, style and function of the cabinet. Brass bullet catches, for instance, would look out of place on an Arts-and-Crafts piece with hand-wrought iron hinges and knobs. Likewise, high-end furniture is no place for plastic-encased magnets or for steel touch latches that are stamped out by the carload.

Catches have functional as well as aesthetic differences, and some catches work better than others on certain kinds of doors. And like everything else, door catches vary in price. Their cost in relation to a piece of furniture is very small, though, so it makes sense to choose exactly the right one.

To help you sort through some of the choices, I have taken a look at a dozen of the most popular door catches. They include commercially available catches and locks, as well as mechanisms built in the shop. In addition to trying these different catches for single doors, I've also found some interesting ways to keep double doors closed, especially in those difficult situations where there is no center divider between the doors.

Magnetic catches

Magnetic catches come in a variety of sizes and shapes and can be used for single or double doors. For large doors, magnetic catches often are used in pairs—at the top and bottom of the door. Most magnetic catches are housed in plastic, which I find objectionable for high-end work. However, there are some small, round magnets (see the photos below left) that mount in holes drilled directly into a door stop or a fixed shelf. This neat installation is more appropriate for better-quality cabinets. Nevertheless, I still don't care for magnetic latches. They're generally ugly, they sound clunky and they can be difficult to fine-tune for just the right amount of holding power.

Touch latches

Touch latches, both mechanical and magnetic, are used most often on kitchen and bathroom cabinets. They also can be used for shop and office furniture. Mechanical touch latches operate with a ratchet and a spring mechanism. When closing the door, the ratchet engages and holds the door closed. Then, when tapped or touched, the ratchet releases, and the spring mechanism pushes the door open. Unlike a mechanical latch, a magnetic touch latch (see the photo below right) uses a magnet on the end of a

Magnetic catches

Touch latches

Bullet catches

tom of the door stile. This way, the bullets wear grooves on the inside edges of the door as opposed to the outside edges of the case frame where they would be visible.

Nothing sounds better than the click of a well-adjusted bullet catch. But these closures can be difficult to adjust and only should be used on small to mid-sized, perfectly flat doors because of their limited holding power. Bullets are appropriate for contemporary furniture as well as shop and office use.

Spinners

Spinners, also called turn buttons or button latches, have a wide range of applications. There are two basic types: exterior and interior. They are low-tech, virtually foolproof and work well in keeping slightly warped doors closed. An exterior spinner (see the left photo on the facing page) consists of a small (usually 1¼ in. to 2 in. long) bar with a hole in the center to take a screw. Spinners are mounted on the face frame next to the door stile. In the horizontal position, the spinner holds the door closed. Turned vertically, the door can be opened. Commercially made spinners usually are brass. Shopmade models can be made of wood. Victorian spinners often had brass backing plates to eliminate wear. Simple spinners are great for shop cabinets; more elaborate versions suit certain period pieces.

Interior spinners (see the top right photos on the facing page) work on the same principle, but they are attached inside the door to the shaft of the door knob. Brass knobs have metal spinners threaded onto the shaft and usually locked in place with a small screw. Wooden knobs have shopmade spinners, usually oval in shape, which are pinned or screwed to the shaft to prevent them from slipping. Cabinets with full face frames are ideal for spinners because the spinner can catch directly behind the frame. Cabinets without face frames require a small groove in the cabinet side for the spinner to lock into. If there is any play between spinner and face frame (or spinner and groove), you can glue in a small tapered shim that will draw the door tighter as the

spring-loaded plunger. Both types require ⅛ in. to ¼ in. of clearance between the door and the doorstop.

I find these latches gimmicky. I use them only on doors that don't get much use, such as secret-compartment panels, because they tend to wear out faster than other types of catches.

Bullet catches

Bullet catches (see the drawing and the photo above) should be used at the top and bottom of doors. These catches have a few drawbacks. They require fine-tuning, they're sensitive to any seasonal changes in the dimensions of the door, and they can't handle warps in the door very well. Even so, they are among my favorite catches because they're unobtrusive and work so well when adjusted correctly. Bullet catches made by Brusso are undoubtedly the best. They are the only ones that have a groove in the strike (or keep) to allow the door to move seasonally. Most other bullet catches have a dimple in the strike, which doesn't allow any seasonal door movement. It is standard procedure to mount the bullets in the case frames and the strikes on the top and bot-

Spinners

spinner closes. Thin plastic washers between the spinner and door and the knob shoulder and door virtually eliminate friction.

Double-ball catches

A variation of the bullet catch is the double-ball catch (see the photo at right). This two-part catch consists of a contoured metal strike that pops between a pair of spring-loaded ball bearings. This is a relatively recent innovation that permits some door movement, allows the holding power to be adjusted and keeps doors from sagging in the closed position.

A word of warning when using double-ball catches: Never mount them in a horizontal position when using solid-wood doors. When mounted vertically, the strike can slide side to side between the two ball bearings, providing $1/4$ in. to $3/8$ in. of movement. However, because there is only $1/64$ in. or so between the strike and the ball housings, mounting this catch horizontally allows for no door movement. Double-ball catches can be particularly difficult to install on single-door cabinets, but they're well-suited to high-end furniture because the holding power can be adjusted for just the right feel when opening the door.

Double-ball catches

Key locks

Key locks

Standard key locks (see the photo above) also can be used to keep doors closed, with or without any other kind of catch. These are most appropriate for little-used doors requiring extra security, because the key must be used each time to open and close the door. Either full- or half-mortise locks can be used. If I go to the trouble of installing a key lock, I use a good one—a three-, four- or even six-lever or tumbler lock. The cheap, single-lever locks aren't worth the effort to install because they can be opened with just a piece of bent wire. On the positive side, a key lock is an attractive visual touch on a cabinet; the downside is that they take time and patience to install correctly.

Closing double doors

Double doors with a center divider can be treated just like single doors. When no divider (or fixed shelf) is present, keeping double doors closed becomes more challenging. The first and easiest choice for inset doors is bullet catches because the catches are mounted above and below the doors and don't need to grab a fixed divider to work.

Another approach I often use is to anchor or fix one door (usually the left one) in place. Then I use it to incorporate one of the catches mentioned in this article to keep the second door closed. How do you anchor a door? There are three simple and readily available pieces of hardware that can be used. One of the easiest to install is a surface-mounted elbow catch (see the top photo on the facing page) that is screwed to the inside of the door, either at the top, bottom or under a fixed shelf. Available in a variety of qualities, these catches can suit everything from a shop-grade cabinet to really high-end work.

Another option for anchoring a door is a pair of surface-mounted sliding bolts screwed to the inside of the door, one at the top and the other at the bottom. Holes need to be drilled into the top door stop and into the bottom shelf-door stop for the bolt barrel. Brass plates mortised into the front edges of the stops make a neat, clean installation. Surface bolts should be sized appropriately for the door. I like solid-brass bolts, even on high-end cabinets.

The third method is a little more costly and time-consuming, but looks more elegant. Flush bolts are mortised into the top and bottom edges of the door stiles. Then latching holes are drilled into the case top and bottom. For solid doors, these holes actually should be elongated slots to allow for door movement. I would use these closures only on top-end cabinets because installation is labor intensive.

Once one door can be locked in place (I usually pick the left one), it can be treated more or less like a divider. I often use an interior wooden spinner on the knob of the other door.

Library catches

Another approach to latching double doors is a library catch (see the drawing and bottom photo on the facing page). This unusual piece of hardware is simple to use once it is properly mortised into the cabinet. It consists of a baseplate with a spring-loaded lever below. When both doors are closed,

Closing double doors

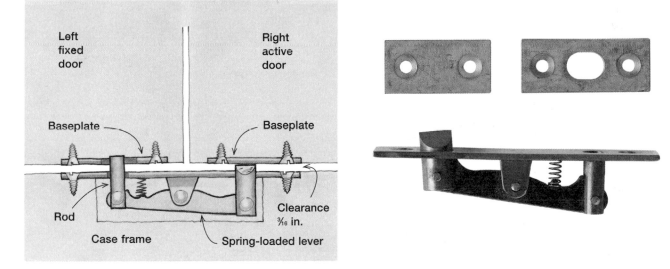

the right (or active) door forces a rod down, pushing another rod on the opposite side of the lever up into the left (fixed) door. The left door remains fixed only as long as the right door is closed. As soon as the right door is opened, the spring retracts the rod and releases the fixed door. To hold the right door closed, use one of the catches suitable for single doors.

For medium and large cabinet doors, a library catch should be installed top and bottom. Clearances above and below the door must be kept to less than $^3/_{16}$ in., or the rods will not engage the door. Library catches are a relatively new type of closure that I've used only a few times. Both my customers and I have been pleased with the results.

SIX

Construction Options for Chairs

Chairmakers are the wizards of woodworking. They seem to have unearthly abilities for joining thin sticks together at odd angles that can support the weight of almost any size person. The best chairmakers' work can withstand tilting back on the rear legs, and other such abuse, without a squeak. The very best work looks good while it stands up to such abuse. Even better are the few that are actually comfortable, too. Notoriously difficult to get right for these reasons, many woodworkers never even attempt a chair in their lifetimes.

Nevertheless, chairs don't need to be impossible projects. They are made of the same materials and joints as other less intimidating furniture. They work on the same principles. The difference is one of degree and complexity. Chairs usually have joinery at angles other than 90°. And no other piece of furniture has to mold itself to the less-than-rectilinear human form. These problems, like all woodworking problems, can be solved by good design. The execution is a question of technique, which is within the ability of any woodworker who can build a jig.

Anyone who has squirmed uncomfortably through a formal dinner party knows the torture a badly designed chair can inflict. Hard flat seats, backs that hit the lumbar region at the wrong angle, arms that leave no purchase for a hand or elbow—the list of possible discomforts from a badly designed chair is long. To remedy this, the Grew-Sheridans came up with an adjustable rig that allows a chair design to be test-fit to individual backs. The rig reduces the calculus of chair design to a simple matter of what feels good and what doesn't. Though not all of us will go to the trouble of building such a rig, the lesson is obvious. Sit in existing chairs, find the ones that feel good, and stick to their proportions when building your own.

Jere Osgood offers some tips on solid engineering. It's crucial to know where a chair takes the most stress, so that those joints can be made strongest and will last a lifetime. How many commercially made chairs end up as firewood because their joints come apart, stretchers break, or they squeak and wobble excessively? The lessons are simple—the trick is to know how chairs take abuse and where the stress concentrates.

DESIGN A CHAIR THAT FITS LIKE A GLOVE

by Glenn Gordon

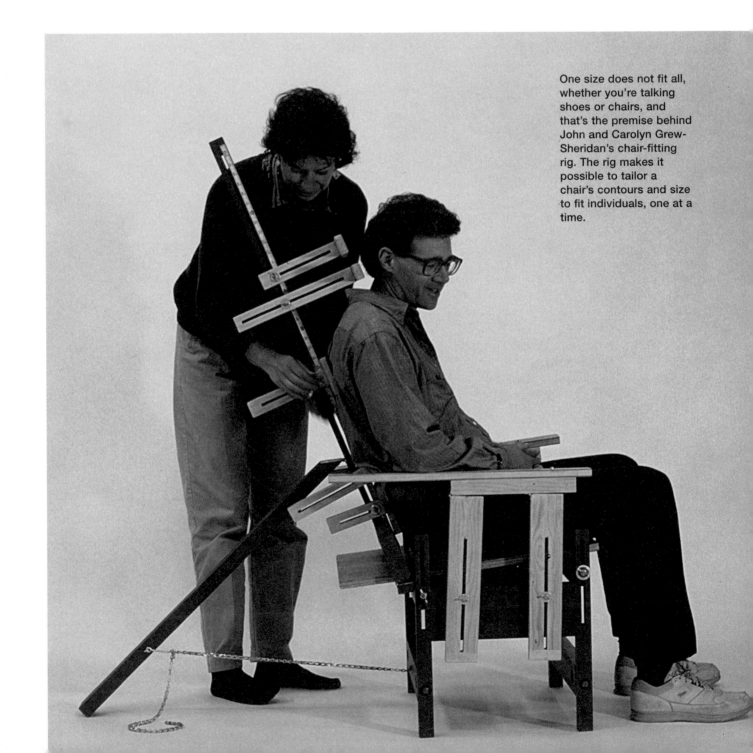

One size does not fit all, whether you're talking shoes or chairs, and that's the premise behind John and Carolyn Grew-Sheridan's chair-fitting rig. The rig makes it possible to tailor a chair's contours and size to fit individuals, one at a time.

"The problem of chair design is considered to be the most demanding in furniture—and for good reasons," says John Grew-Sheridan, who has thought about it a lot. Structural integrity is critical, even more so than for other furniture. At the same time, a chair must be comfortable and pleasing to the senses. The world has no shortage of ugly chairs that are comfortable or pretty chairs that aren't, so we have plenty of evidence that combining strength, comfort and comeliness in one design is not without its difficulties. San Francisco furnituremakers Carolyn and John Grew-Sheridan have worked out an approach to chair design that ensures a chair will be comfortable while demonstrating that "the dictates of comfort need not interfere with aesthetic considerations because," as John says, "there are an infinite number of ways to connect the critical structural and support points of a chair."

The Grew-Sheridans have been making chairs since 1975, and teaching others how to make them since 1980, when the University of California invited the couple to give a seminar on the subject. In preparing for the seminar, the Grew-Sheridans designed an adjustable rig for measuring individuals for custom-fitted chairs (see the photo on the facing page) and developed an inexpensive way of making full-scale mockups of their designs. Using the adjustable rig, they determine various chair dimensions, plot them as points on a graph and then transfer the coordinates onto a perspective drawing grid (available from art-supply stores). The result is a skeletal perspective sketch, or stick figure of the chair, showing all the critical dimensional relationships but still devoid of any form or structure (see the drawing above).

After working through the aesthetic and structural aspects of a chair's design on tracing paper over the grid, the Grew-Sheridans next make a full-scale model of the chair by laminating ordinary corrugated cardboard into "lumber" with thinned white glue, shaping the cardboard lumber into chair parts and hot gluing the "joints" (see the top photo). This technique allows them to make modifications with a minimum of effort, saving wood, money and grief.

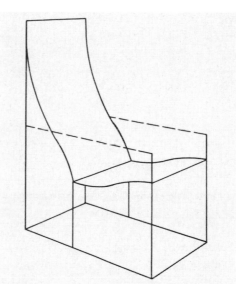

From plotted points to cardboard mockup to finished chair, the Grew-Sheridan's process not only ensures that a chair will fit its owner perfectly but also that the chair's design will have been considered from every perspective, not just side and front views. Designing a chair in the round and building a prototype almost guarantees a better-looking chair.

From the general to the specific

The Grew-Sheridans gathered their information on essential body measurements for chair design from two publications. Most works on ergonomics, in trying to get to the bottom of seating comfort scientifically, proceed from an engineering mentality that tends to pay serious technical attention to everything except the seat of the pants. However, there are two classics in the field that Carolyn and John say they find tremendously useful. The first, a homely little pamphlet without the slightest aspiration to scientific importance, is called *Basic Design Measurements for Sitting* (by Clara Ridder, University of Arkansas, Agricultural Experiment Station, Fayetteville, Ark., 1959). The second is *Humanscale 1/2/3* (by

Niels Diffrient et al., Cambridge, Mass., The MIT Press, 1978), a portfolio containing a booklet and three cleverly laid-out plastic reference cards with rotating dials. Turning these dials reveals all sorts of biometric data through numerous windows cut into the plastic cards. All the parts of the Grew-Sheridan's rig were sized, and the ranges for its various adjustments determined, from data in these two publications. The rig can accommodate just about any size human being, from the tiniest nymph to a nose tackle the size of a bison.

The beauty of the Grew-Sheridan's rig is its specificity because ideal chair dimensions—based on averages—exist only on paper. When a class of the Grew-Sheridan's chairmaking students averaged all

Fitting the chair to the customer

by Carolyn and John Grew-Sheridan

The first step in the fitting process is to measure the person sitting on a plain flat bench. This provides a set of starting measurements of the person's body that we can transfer to the rig. We're careful to make absolutely clear to the person we're fitting that this is only a preliminary setting or starting point. We've found if we don't emphasize this point, often people will refrain from telling us that the seat-to-back angle's too acute or the thoracic support is too low. We try to loosen them up and get them involved in the fitting process.

Taking measurements

The first measurement, known as the popliteal, is taken by measuring from the floor to the underside of the thigh at the knee. The customer should have on the same shoes that will typically be worn when sitting in the chair. Then we measure from that same point in the crook of the knee to the surface of the back. Next, holding a yardstick against the person's back with the end of the yardstick on the bench, we measure the height of the waist. We determine the location of the waist by having the customer bend to the side while seated. As it turns out, if you carry the waist measurement around to the back, that's just about where most people like to feel lumbar support.

We measure from seat to elbow to determine armrest height and note the relaxed spread of the arms as well for the width of the armrest at the elbows. The angle of the armrest is less predictable, we've found, so we just experiment until we hit upon a comfortable angle. Next, we measure from the seat to the underarm. This measurement is required for dining chairs in particular because it tells you approximately where to position upper back support.

Just as a dining chair requires upper back support, each type of chair has its own special traits and requirements. All chairs need to be wide enough in the seat—obviously—to get in and out of, so we take a seated hip width measurement; shoulder width isn't that significant a measurement unless you're building a chair that will partially envelop its owner, such as a large stuffed chair or recliner. Nevertheless, while we're measuring, we get all the information we can; there's no telling when a client we're fitting for a reading chair will want to order a set of dining chairs.

The final two vertical measurements that we take are from the seat to the nape of the neck and from the seat to the back of the head. These measurements are most critical for a chair designed primarily for relaxing in, where head support is essential.

Next, with the yardstick (or some other straight edge) still in place against the person's back and the person sitting up straight, we measure the horizontal distance from straight edge to lumbar (waist

their own measurements together and set up the rig accordingly, the result wasn't comfortable for a single person in the class. The chair industry (one size fits all) necessarily has to work to a happy medium, which will inevitably entail a certain amount of individual unhappiness. The Grew-Sheridans, meanwhile, have worked out a way for a custom chairmaker to make people happy, one at a time.

Finding and mapping a fit

The first step in the Grew-Sheridan's fitting procedure is to get a series of rough measurements of the person for whom the chair is being designed (see the sidebar below for a detailed explanation of the fitting process). These initial measurements are taken with the person seated not in the rig but on a flat picnic bench or anything similar. The Grew-Sheridans then make preliminary adjustments to the rig based on those initial measurements and ask the person to have a seat. With the person seated in the rig, the Grew-Sheridans proceed to refine the rig's adjustments. Working by trial and error, and relying on their experience, they first establish an optimal seat depth, height and angle to the floor (in that order), and then they establish the height of the armrests (when appropriate) and the angle of the back to the seat. Then they adjust the series of back supports on the back rail, working from bottom (sacral support) to top (head support).

When all adjustments have been made so that the rig feels right to the sitter, the set-

measurement transferred to the back), then from straight edge to the juncture of head and neck (the nape) and last, from straight edge to the back of the head.

Adjusting the rig

Setting the rig is straightforward once we've got all the above measurements (see the drawing on the facing page for information on where various parts of the rig are adjusted). The measurements and angles vary for different kinds of chairs, but for the sake of explanation, let's presuppose we're designing a reading chair. (Information on the requirements for various types of chairs can be found in the book, *Basic Design Measurements for Sitting,* mentioned above.) We set the seat depth first to about 2 in. less than the measured under-thigh length and then set the seat height at the knee to about 3 in. less than the popliteal measurement. We drop the rear of the seat 3 in. from the front setting (or 5 in. from the popliteal). We set the arm width at the elbow next (this generally falls in a fairly narrow range—between 21 in. and 23 in.) and then set the arm height at the elbow about 1 in. to 2 in. greater than the seat-to-elbow measurement.

For this preliminary setting, we position the back at 105° to the seat. Since we're adjusting the rig to fit the customer, this seat-to-back angle will often change. If we run out of range as we're adjusting the settings of the back supports, we can change the seat-to-back angle.

We adjust all the back supports using the measurements just taken, beginning with the sacral (1 in. forward of the back rail, 3 in. up from the seat). Proceeding up the back, we adjust the lumbar support—probably the most important—(usually 8 in. to 10 in. up, 1 in. to 2 in. forward of the back rail), thoracic support (set at the height of the underarm, at the same distance from the back rail as the sacral adjustment) and, finally, the neck and head supports. These last adjustments vary widely: a survey of 55 of our former and current chairbuilding students revealed a vertical range of 14 in.

From this point on, it's really just a question of using your common sense and making increasingly finer adjustments. The chair's intended use, how it will relate to other furnishings (such as a dining or end table) and whether the chair's owner wears heels, flats, sneakers (or is barefoot) all need to be considered when translating the information gathered on the rig into a chair design. When we schedule a fitting, we encourage the customer to bring whatever is necessary to make the fitting absolutely realistic. That might mean a pair of slippers and a book or a newspaper—or even a bowl, spoon, box of corn flakes and a quart of milk. Pretending to eat a bowl of cereal while reading the paper just isn't the same as actually doing it, and we want the chair to be comfortable in use.

tings of the rig (in side view) are plotted on graph paper, along with distances measured from the floor to various points on the body (to determine a horizontal reference). Connect the dots, and you have a side view of a chair—or, more accurately, not of the chair itself, but of the "comfort-curve" for the person being fitted.

The next step is to render that view in a three-quarter front view using a perspective grid, as shown in the drawing on the facing page. This provides a three-dimensional skeletal view of the chair, a perspective armature over which can be drawn, on tracing paper, any number of structural and stylistic variations. Every chair sketched will be in scale, will show the correct curves and angle for the back, and will have the seat the right height and angle off the floor. Each variant drawn will be the same size and depicted from the same point of view as all the rest for clear, side-by-side comparisons.

From paper to prototype

The Grew-Sheridan's adjustable rig can help a designer resolve questions about a chair's size, proportions and comfort, but neither the rig nor the perspective sketches generated with it can give you a realistic representation of the chair in the round. A perspective sketch can take you part of the way, but it's easy to ruin lumber: If you have a change of heart about a detail halfway through building a chair, it can cost you.

It's helpful, therefore—before you cut any stock—to see what a chair will look like in three dimensions. One way to do that is to make a scale model. A better way is to make a full-size mock-up. The Grew-Sheridan's technique for making full-size mock-ups is quick, cheap and surprisingly effective at evoking the look of the finished chair. The material they use—corrugated cardboard, found just about anywhere—usually for free—has good modeling properties: body, thickness and even a certain amount of strength. Using thinned white glue, they laminate the cardboard to whatever dimension of stock they need, then draw the pattern for, say, a chair arm on it, and bandsaw it out just as though they were working a

piece of wood. They then use disc sanders, rasps and files to shape the arm, which goes quickly because the corrugated cardboard is really mostly air. Because the material is so easily worked and can usually be had for nothing, there's no reluctance to experiment.

Form follows function

Practicality, directness and an economy of means characterize the Grew-Sheridan's work as chairmakers. Their premise as designers is reflected in some passages John quotes from *Form and Function,* by Horace Greenough, first published in 1843: "The most beautiful chairs," wrote Greenough, "invite you by a promise of ease, and they keep that promise; they bear neither flowers nor dragons nor idle displays of the turner's caprice."

"Greenough was searching for great principles of construction," explained Carolyn. "He argued that one should first look at the use and only then turn to the decorative elements. He believed the conflict in design is between the essential and the pretentious." In other words, everything in the design of an object, whether it's a canoe or a shoe or a chair, ought to be subordinate to function. If this idea is respected—if function is clearly understood and sympathetically addressed and the consciousness of it extended to such considerations as the chair's interaction with the sitter's body, the finish of the wood, the feel of the fabrics, the intention in the flare of the curves—form will flow from it. The most comfortable (and the most beautiful) chairs aren't conceived as cakes to be decorated with a pastry tube. The beauty of a chair—whether it's the ancient Greek Klismos chair or one of Hans Wegner's contemporary pieces—comes instead from the character of its response to structural necessity. They maintain a tradition in the design of functional objects in which practicality and beauty aren't at odds but are rather in equilibrium—are, in fact, one and the same, a tradition that John and Carolyn Grew-Sheridan are helping to sustain.

Adjustable chair-fitting rig

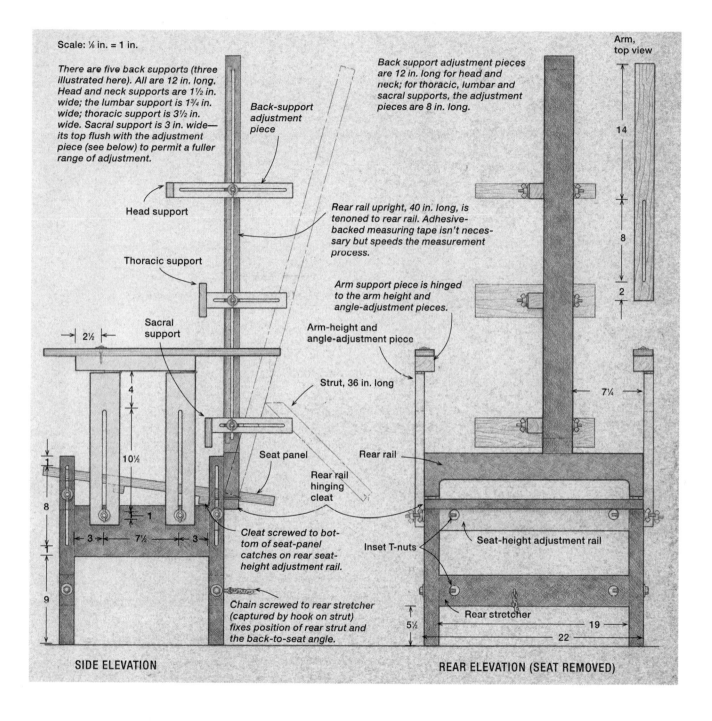

Scale: ⅛ in. = 1 in.

There are five back supports (three illustrated here). All are 12 in. long. Head and neck supports are 1½ in. wide; the lumbar support is 1¾ in. wide; thoracic support is 3½ in. wide. Sacral support is 3 in. wide—its top flush with the adjustment piece (see below) to permit a fuller range of adjustment.

Head support

Thoracic support

Sacral support

Back-support adjustment piece

2½

4

10½

1

3

7½

3

1

8

9

Seat panel

Cleat screwed to bottom of seat-panel catches on rear seat-height adjustment rail.

Chain screwed to rear stretcher (captured by hook on strut) fixes position of rear strut and the back-to-seat angle.

SIDE ELEVATION

Back support adjustment pieces are 12 in. long for head and neck; for thoracic, lumbar and sacral supports, the adjustment pieces are 8 in. long.

Rear rail upright, 40 in. long, is tenoned to rear rail. Adhesive-backed measuring tape isn't necessary but speeds the measurement process.

Arm support piece is hinged to the arm height and angle-adjustment pieces.

Arm-height and angle-adjustment piece

Strut, 36 in. long

Rear rail

Rear rail hinging cleat

Inset T-nuts

Arm, top view

14

8

2

7¼

Seat-height adjustment rail

Rear stretcher

5½

19

22

REAR ELEVATION (SEAT REMOVED)

WHAT MAKES A CHAIR STAND UP TO ABUSE?

by Jere Osgood

Nearly 40 years ago when I was learning how to make furniture, my fellow students and I spent a lot of time designing chairs. Whenever we finished one, our instructor, Tage Frid, would sit in the chair. "Sit" isn't the right word. He would land on it hard, tip it onto its back legs and wiggle around to see if it was going to fall apart. I never saw a chair break, but I witnessed a lot of sweating students.

Another Scandinavian furniture maker, the Swedish designer Carl Malmsten, once said that chairs are "the most difficult member of the furniture family to master." I think this is true. A chair, especially a dining chair, bears burdens unlike any other piece of furniture in a home. Its successful design depends as much on solid engineering as it does on aesthetic sensibility. To build a dining chair that is both beautiful and strong requires careful attention to the forces working against it.

What are those forces? First and foremost, a chair supports a person many times its own weight. This weight comes and goes, moves and shifts.

Different parts of a chair experience stress and strain at different times. Secondly, as Tage Frid illustrated to us, the weight is deposited on a chair with force, not gently and gradually, so it must be able to withstand these moments of impact. Chairs also get dragged around the house for all sorts of purposes, from eating and lounging to working and sometimes even changing a light bulb. Few pieces of furniture work this hard.

Every chair design accommodates these forces in different ways, making it difficult to establish ground rules that can be applied to all. Most wooden chairs, however, share a few critical connections holding the seat and legs together. The success of these joints will, in large part, determine whether a chair design will stand or fall after years of use.

It looks good, but will it hold up? Behind the lissome lines of this chair is a carefully engineered skeleton designed to withstand the substantial force of a 200-pound dinner guest.

Seat rails carry the load

When Tage Frid dropped himself onto a chair, he would push his weight into the back, sometimes tilting onto the rear legs. You may be doing this right now as you read this article. If you are, notice how the back becomes a lever when you lean into it. This weight exerts tremendous force on the intersection between the back and the seat, pushing these pieces apart. Not surprisingly, this is one of the most important joints in a chair (see drawing on p. 173). If this joint is poorly designed—and I know this from experience—the seat rail will work loose from the back leg. It may not collapse, but the chair will soon wiggle.

In most wooden chairs (other than Windsor-style chairs) the seat rails have tenons that fit into mortises in the back legs. The tenon has to withstand the weight of the sitter as well as side-to-side racking forces. Therefore it must be thick—at least $3/8$ inch but I prefer to make them closer to

$1/2$ inch. I have seen tenons that were too small simply snap off. To get the most mechanical advantage, the depth of the tenon should be more than half the width of the back leg.

Another important consideration is the glue. Today more than ever we rely on adhesives to hold a chair together. This makes it possible to build strong chairs with less material, but it also means maximizing the strength of the bond. One way to compare different joinery options is to measure the total area of the long-grain gluing surface. I measure the long-grain faces of the tenon and the corresponding sides of the mortise and compare different joints to see which has the most gluing surface.

Chair joinery is a balancing act, though. A large tenon with lots of gluing surface will be stronger than a smaller one, but it also means that more material must be removed from the back leg to make the mortise. A gaping mortise in the back leg may fatally weaken its strength, defeating the purpose of the strong tenon. If the chair has a rear seat rail mortised into the back legs at the same spot, this will weaken the leg even further.

One solution is to make haunched or "webbed" tenons that are either T-shaped or U-shaped (see the drawing on the facing page). This reduces the size of the mortise without sacrificing the length of the tenon. Although there is less gluing area, it still makes a strong joint. Another way around this dilemma is to attach the rear seat rail to the side seat rails just inside the back legs using stub tenons, but not so close as to interfere with the roots of the side rail tenon (see the top right drawing on p. 175). I can then run the back slats past the seat and either attach them into a lower stretcher or directly into the back legs.

The dimensions of the rails are as critical as the joints. No amount of joinery will help a chair survive years of use if the rails are too small. Width is more critical than thickness, because the rails must withstand tension and compression forces. A chair I made 40 years ago has rails that are plenty thick—nearly two inches—but the width is far too narrow and the joint has failed (see the top photo on p. 172). I have found that the seat rail should be at least $3^1/2$ inches from top to bottom where it meets the back leg, especially if the chair has no stretchers.

Finally, the rear seat joints are stressed the most when someone tilts a chair onto its back legs. As an insurance policy, I try to position the bottom of the back legs further behind the seat than the top. The more the legs angle back, the harder it is to tip the chair onto the rear legs. There is a side benefit to doing this: The legs keep the top of the chair from scraping against a wall. If the legs are angled too far back, though, they become a tripping hazard.

The forces working against a chair

People land hard in a chair, so the joints must be strong enough to withstand this stress. In this basic chair design, the strength of the joints between the seat rails and legs is critical. Improperly designed, the joints work loose and the chair wiggles.

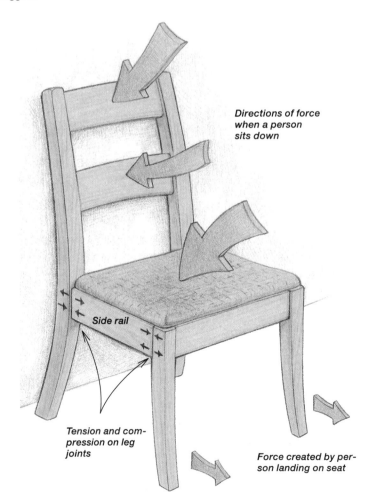

Directions of force when a person sits down

Side rail

Tension and compression on leg joints

Force created by person landing on seat

Seat rails work the hardest

The joints between the side seat rails and the back legs bear the brunt of the weight. The top of the joint, under tension, is being pried apart by the force of someone leaning back. The bottom is in compression and will help resist this force.

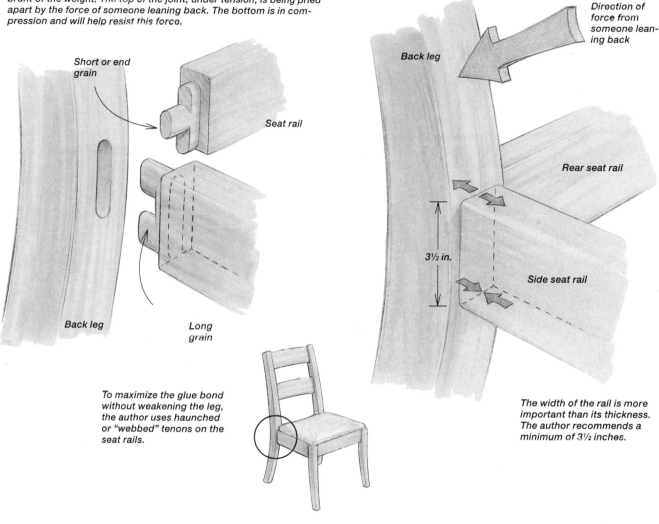

Short or end grain

Seat rail

Back leg

Long grain

Direction of force from someone leaning back

Back leg

Rear seat rail

3½ in.

Side seat rail

To maximize the glue bond without weakening the leg, the author uses haunched or "webbed" tenons on the seat rails.

The width of the rail is more important than its thickness. The author recommends a minimum of 3½ inches.

Front legs absorb some of the strain

The back leg-to-seat rail connection may bear the brunt of a 200-pound dinner guest, but I have seen a lot of broken front legs, too. When someone sits down in a chair, the weight pushes the front leg out, making the joint between the front leg and the seat rail work hard to stay tight (see the drawing on facing page). A strong joint in front fights this tendency. If this joint is weak, everything relies on the strength of that back joint.

For many years I have used a sliding dovetail to counterbalance the weight that pushes the front leg out (see the drawing and photo on p. 176). The dovetail is locked in place by the tenon on the front seat rail, creating a mechanical joint that has proven indestructible. With stronger glues, this may seem extreme, but I like insurance. It's not always possible to use a dovetail, but when you get the chance, take it. A locked dovetail is stronger than a mortise-and-tenon, and it will work even if the glue fails.

Corner blocks complete the seat frame. These small blocks, fastened to the inside of the seat rails, reinforce the joinery and provide a convenient spot to drive a screw into an upholstered seat frame. One word of advice: Don't rely on the seat itself to keep a

Bigger doesn't always mean stronger, as the author illustrates with this chair he made in the 1950s. The seat rails are plenty thick, but strength comes from width, not thickness. These rails were too narrow and wiggled loose over the years.

Trim back the tenons to minimize the amount of material cut out of the leg for the mortises. Both the side and rear rails shown here have ample long-grain gluing surface.

chair rigid. A woven or upholstered seat may help tie things together at first, but seats invariably loosen with wear. If the chair is designed properly it should hold together with or without the seat.

Strength in stretchers

The easiest way to strengthen a chair is by increasing the bulk of the parts, both the rails and the legs. While this method can sometimes overcome engineering deficiencies, it usually results in a heavy, clunky chair that may not break, but isn't very inviting. One way to gain strength without sacrificing delicacy is by spreading the load among a greater number of parts.

A stretcher system below the seat, for instance, will help resist twisting and rack-

More than one way to connect the back legs _____

In many chairs, the back legs are connected by a seat rail, which is often mortised into the leg at the same spot as the side rails. Moving the rear seat rail so it spans between the two side rails means fewer mortises in the back leg. Corner blocks reinforce the joints and provide a secure place to anchor a slip seat.

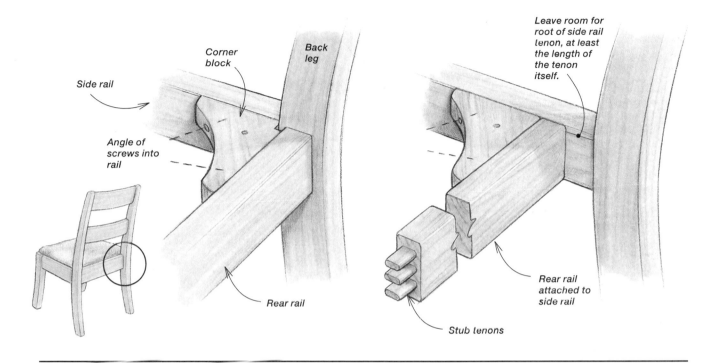

Side rail

Corner block

Back leg

Angle of screws into rail

Rear rail

Leave room for root of side rail tenon, at least the length of the tenon itself.

Rear rail attached to side rail

Stub tenons

---

ing forces on the legs, reinforcing the seat joints (see the drawings on p. 177). Shaker chairs often have several sets of turned stretchers encircling the legs. These chairs are quite strong, yet each individual turning is light and delicate. To achieve the same strength without stretchers would mean bulking up the seat frame, which would change the design.

Adding arms to a chair does the same thing as adding stretchers, although the strength is up higher where it can help stabilize the back as well as the legs. The crest rail also holds the chair together and helps keep the back legs in alignment.

Strength comes at a price, though, and you may not want to pay it. I like to tuck my feet underneath the seat, for example, so stretchers down to the floor would not suit me. Instead, I might make the stretchers a little bigger but use fewer of them, keeping the chair strong while leaving more legroom underneath.

Anatomy of a dining chair _____

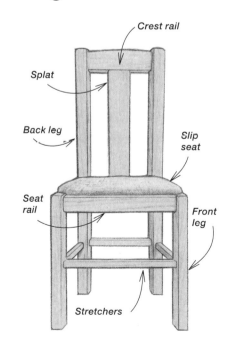

Crest rail

Splat

Back leg

Slip seat

Seat rail

Front leg

Stretchers

Sliding dovetails keep on working even if the glue fails. Corner blocks reinforce the joint and serve as a good place to fasten an upholstered seat.

Dovetail locks the front leg

The author uses a sliding dovetail to fasten the side rail to the front leg. The dovetail is locked in place by the tenon from the front rail.

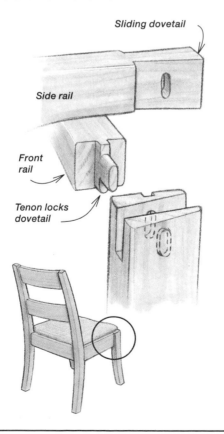

Sliding dovetail

Side rail

Front rail

Tenon locks dovetail

A solution that I like to use is a split side rail and stretcher combination. The lower part of the rail becomes a stretcher and meets the front leg about 5 inches below the seat rail, counteracting some of the tension on the front leg. In this case the joinery at the back leg has proven to be quite strong, which is why I have the lower stretcher curve into the seat rail at the back of the chair. It also makes the design more fluid and less rectilinear.

There are countless ways to counteract the forces working against a chair. The classic Thonet cafe chair is completely different from a Shaker ladderback. However you choose to address these structural problems, I strongly recommend full-size shop drawings and a full-size pine mockup. These are good places to analyze the joinery and engineering.

Structure and joinery are only two elements of any design. For me, making a chair is more about design than engineering. Comfort and style are far more important to most people. So durability has to be weighed against delicacy. Strength against comfort. Weight against beauty. Engineering is just one of the pieces to the puzzle.

Stretchers keep the legs in check _____

The author uses a sliding dovetail to fasten the side rail to the front leg. The dovetail is locked in place by the tenon from the front rail.

Box stretcher
Shaker chairs often have delicate turnings, which means more parts are required to carry the load.

H-stretcher
The stretcher between the front legs is replaced by one connecting the two side stretchers, adding more room below.

Osgood's split-rail stretcher
The rail splits to reinforce the front leg down low, where the extra support is needed.

Arms act like upper stretchers
Arms tie the legs together and reinforce the joint between the back and the seat.

ABOUT THE AUTHORS

Niall Barrett, a self-taught woodworker who has been building commission furniture for 20 years, was raised in Ireland. He currently owns and operates Avalon Studios, a custom cabinetmaking shop in Narrowsburg, N.Y. He is also the author of *Bookcases.*

Joe Beals makes bespoke furniture and architectural millwork in Marshfield, Mass. He is self-taught, about which he makes this comment: "Learning by mistakes is a painful education, but no other method concentrates the attention so perfectly." He also writes fiction and plays traditional Irish music on the fiddle.

Christian Becksvoort is a long-time cabinetmaker in the Shaker style and a contributing editor to *Fine Woodworking* magazine. He is the author of *The Shaker Legacy.*

Graham Blackburn built his first house in Woodstock, N.Y., in 1968 and wrote his first book in 1974. Since then he has written and illustrated many books and articles on various aspects of building and woodworking, including *Furniture By Design* and *Traditional Woodworking Handtools.* He has a website at www.blackburnbooks.com

John Gallagher builds furniture in Elkins, W.Va. He has also built stringed instruments and hewn-log houses.

Glenn Gordon has designed and built furniture since 1970. He has written and photographed woodworking articles for several magazines and has been a contributing editor to *Woodwork* since 1993. He lives in St. Paul, Minn.

John Grew Sheridan is an acclaimed and innovative furnituremaker, designer, sculptor, photographer, writer, and anti-war Vietnam War veteran with a light teaching schedule. He was partners with **Carolyn Grew-Sheridan** in Grew-Sheridan Studios until her death in 1996. Their work has been on display at the Renwick Gallery of the Smithsonian.

Garrett Hack opened his own shop in 1973 and later studied furnituremaking at Boston University's Program in Artisanry. He designs and builds furniture in Vermont and is a regular contributor to *Fine Woodworking* magazine. He is the author of *The Handplane Book* and *Classic Hand Tools.*

Paul Harrell is a furnituremaker in Pitsboro, N.C. He studied under James Krenov at the College of the Redwoods in Fort Bragg, Calif.

Bill Keyser is a professor of woodworking and furniture design at the Rochester Institute of Technology. He also designs and builds custom furniture on commission.

Will Neptune is a furnituremaker and a woodworking instructor at the North Bennet Street School in Boston.

Jere Osgood has been a furniture designer and craftsman since 1957. He grew up on Staten Island, N.Y., and studied furniture-making at the Rochester Institute of Technology and in Denmark. His work has been purchased by public collections, including the Museum of Fine Arts in Boston, and he was named a Fellow by the American Craft Council. He now teaches short courses around the country, in addition to making furniture in his studio in Wilton, N.H.

Gary Rogowski has been building furniture in Portland, Oreg., since 1974. His design work has been shown in galleries nationwide. A contributing editor to *Fine Woodworking* magazine and the author of *Router Joinery,* he has taught classes and workshops around the country. He now operates his own school, the Northwest Woodworking Studio, which promotes an appreciation of the craft through hands-on education.

Ed Speas is a woodworker living in Cumming, Ga.

Jim Tolpin is a writer and woodworker in Port Townsend, Wash. He is the author of many books, including *Working at Woodworking, Traditional Kitchen Cabinets, The Toolbox Book, The New Cottage Home,* and *The New Family Home.*

John Wagner is the author of *Building Adirondack Furniture.* He lives in Montpelier, Vt., where he writes frequently on building technology issues.

Stephen Winchester started woodworking as a carpenter's apprentice in 1972. Now, he has his own shop, where he makes custom furniture and teaches an apprentice. Though he never took a formal woodworking course, he considers the pages of *Fine Woodworking* his classroom. He and his wife are currently restoring a Victorian farmhouse in Gilmanton, N.H.

CREDITS

Vince Babak (illustrator): 32, 33, 36

Christian Becksvoort (photographer): 134

Jonathan Binzen (photographer): 2, 4, 14, 17, 19-21, 40, 41

Graham Blackburn (illustrator): 124-129

Giatti Designs, Inc. (photographer): 46

William Duckworth (photographer): 144-149

Chuck Fuhrer (photographer): 132, 134

John Gallagher (illustrator): 16, 17

Michael Gellatly (illustrator): 60, 62-67

Glenn Gordon (photographer): 164, 165

Carolyn Grew-Sheridan (photographer): 165

Boyd Hagan (photographer): 69, 70, 72-76, 156-158, 160, 161

Phil Harris (photographer): 97

Sloan Howard (photographer): 38, 52, 54-57

Seth Janovsky (photographer): 18

Heather Lambert (illustrator): 92, 93, 95, 169

Tom Langenderfer (illustrator): 136, 138, 139, 143

Bob LaPointe (illustrator): 41-45, 70, 72-75, 106, 108, 109, 110, 112, 172, 173, 175-177

Vincent Laurence (photographer): 22, 31, 33-36, 77, 78, 80, 83-85, 87, 89, 98, 99, 102, 106, 108, 113, 116, 117, 120, 121, 123, 153-155

David Leveille (illustrator): 8-12

Rick Longenecher (photographer): 130

Maria Meleschnig (illustrator): 48, 54-57, 119, 121-123

Scott Phillips (photographer): 6, 7, 10-13

Dean Powell (photographer): 162, 170, 171, 174, 176

Strother Purdy (photographer): 114, 135, 138-142

Jim Richey (illustrator): 102, 103, 151-155

Charley Robinson (photographer): 58, 91, 94, 159, 161

William Sampson (photographer): 24-29

John Thoe (photographer): 132

Dan Thornton (illustrator): 86, 88

Jim Tolpin (photographer): 47, 51

John Wagner (photographer): 53

Mathew Wells (illustrator): 131, 133, 158, 161

Craig Wester (photographer): 105

EQUIVALENCE CHART

Inches	Centimeters	Millimeters	Inches	Centimeters	Millimeters
$\frac{1}{8}$	0.3	3	12	30.5	305
$\frac{1}{4}$	0.6	6	13	33.0	330
$\frac{3}{8}$	1.0	10	14	35.6	356
$\frac{1}{2}$	1.3	13	15	38.1	381
$\frac{5}{8}$	1.6	16	16	40.6	406
$\frac{3}{4}$	1.9	19	17	43.2	432
$\frac{7}{8}$	2.2	22	18	45.7	457
1	2.5	25	19	48.3	483
$1\frac{1}{4}$	3.2	32	20	50.8	508
$1\frac{1}{2}$	3.8	38	21	53.3	533
$1\frac{3}{4}$	4.4	44	22	55.9	559
2	5.1	51	23	58.4	584
$2\frac{1}{2}$	6.4	64	24	61.0	610
3	7.6	76	25	63.5	635
$3\frac{1}{2}$	8.9	89	26	66.0	660
4	10.2	102	27	68.6	686
$4\frac{1}{2}$	11.4	114	28	71.1	711
5	12.7	127	29	73.7	737
6	15.2	152	30	76.2	762
7	17.8	178	31	78.7	787
8	20.3	203	32	81.3	813
9	22.9	229	33	83.8	838
10	25.4	254	34	86.4	864
11	27.9	279	35	88.9	889
			36	91.4	914

INDEX

Publisher: Jim Childs

Associate Publisher: Helen Albert

Associate Editor: Strother Purdy

Designer: Amy Bernard Russo

Layout Artist: Carol Petro

Indexer: Harriet Hodges

Fine Woodworking magazine

Editor: Timothy D. Schreiner

Art Director: Bob Goodfellow

Managing Editor: Jefferson Kolle

Senior Editors: Jonathan Binzen, Anatole Burkin

Associate Editor: William Duckworth

Assistant Editor: Matthew Teague

Associate Art Director: Michael Pekovich